# When Life Goes

# From Cruise Control To Out Of Control

## Jim Garnett

ZIKLAG PUBLISHERS

—

# Table of Contents

—

—

# Foreword

"I take care of you, not your boss."

That statement was made in July 2011 and was the beginning of a cycle in our lives that has continued now for over two years. It has been a cycle in which we have learned more about God and His ability to sustain us, than we had known heretofore.

Don't write me off as a nut job just yet, but that statement was made by God to me in the middle of the night as I was struggling with a situation at work. Did I actually hear a voice speaking to me out loud? Of course not. It was the still small voice of the Holy Spirit communicating with me in the depths of my spirit.

Having been a pastor for almost 30 years, I believe theologically and practically that God communicates with His children. Jesus said in John 10, *"My sheep listen to my voice; I know them and they follow me"* (John 10:27 NIV). And the Psalmist wrote, *"The Lord confides in those who fear Him"* (Psalm 25:14 NIV)

Basically, God's voice is heard by those who know Him as Shepherd as they read His Word, the Bible. God can also communicate to us through other methods, like Divinely ordered circumstances, Christian counsel, and the leading of the Holy Spirit. But these other methods must always coincide with the Bible, never contradict it. In other words, God will never lead us contrary to His written Word.

A problem had arisen at work, and I did not know exactly how to handle it. My boss was very upset because he felt I had charged him too much for an order of my financial booklets. He had been ordering these 26 page booklets from me for over

—

ten years, and used them to supplement our financial education efforts. I had served as his Education Director for 15 years and had written this booklet as one of a four-book series called SmartStartz for our state's Credit Union League.

I had just been made aware that my boss thought he owned these booklets because I had written them while an employee of his company. But these booklets were written under contract with the Credit Union League. My employer had nothing to do with the origination or ownership of these booklets. My ownership of the copyrights was part of the contract agreement.

To my amazement, he was contending that he should have paid only the printing cost with no mark up at all. Understand, he was not saying that I charged him too much profit, but that I should not have charged him any profit at all!

At this point in time, I had authored seven books on various topics concerning financial management and family counseling. I had never sold any book for just the cost of printing. People who write books deserve to make a profit for their efforts.

The invoice was paid as billed, but I was uncomfortable thinking that there could be hard feelings over this in the future. As a financial counselor, I had seen many relationships ruined over money issues.

So, after receiving payment, I began to pray and ask God what I should do. I knew I had not done anything deceptive or devious, and had solid legal footing for my ownership of the material.

I considered giving him back the profit I had made on the last order, but I knew that he might take that as an admission of guilt, so I wasn't sure just what to do.

—

I struggled with the issue all weekend, and about 3AM Sunday morning I awakened and sat up on the edge of my bed. I knew that God had answered my prayer and was directing me to return the profit for the last order to the company.

With that direction from the Lord, came this statement, "I take care of you, not your boss." I silently said, "Ok" to the Lord and went back to sleep. The next day I wrote him a check for $3000 to return the profit I had made on the 7000 booklets he ordered.

I would like to tell you that he accepted the check graciously, but he still seemed very upset and did not appear to appreciate my gesture to settle the issue with integrity. But I did what I felt God wanted me to do and decided to trust God to "take care of me" like He said He would do.

Looking back, I see now that God was preparing me for what He was preparing me for. That statement "I take care of you" was a phrase that would embed itself in my heart as we began a journey of heartache and loss like we had never experienced before.

These writings are not meant to focus mainly on the difficulties, but to focus on the amazing ways God proved Himself to us to be faithful in the midst of the difficulties.

This cycle has continued over two years now, and I can say with absolute assurance: God has "taken care of us."

*Jim Garnett*

—

# Part One

## *"Ziklag" Becomes A Household Word*

# 1. Ziklag: A Place Of Long Ago

Had you mentioned the name "Ziklag" a couple of years ago, I would have shrugged my shoulders and said, "What is Ziklag – I don't think I've ever heard of it?"

If you asked me today, I would tell you that "Ziklag" is a place that God has made very precious to my wife, Ginny, and me. It is the place where you are taught what God can do when you have come to the complete end of what you can do for yourself.

If I said that I hope you never have to visit Ziklag, I would not be telling you the truth. It is a terrible place. It is a lonely place. It is a place that none of us would ever choose to go if the choosing were up to us (most likely why God does not give us a "vote" in the matter).

Simply put, Ziklag is the name of the place where the promises of God are introduced to our greatest problems. A time in which we come to the complete end of what we can do, and begin to learn what God can do.

Ziklag is the place that God said to us, "My dear children, I know you are at the end of your road. I know you have no strength left, and I know you have no place to turn, but I will be your strength, I will be your hope, and I will be your peace. Just remember Ziklag and it will turn your sorrow into song."

Ziklag was an ancient Biblical city in the semi-desert region of southern Israel. Its importance lies in the fact that it is associated with King David, Israel's greatest king. Its place in history is recorded in 1 Samuel 27-30.

It was occupied by the Philistines when David, and those loyal to him, fled to hide from King Saul. Achish, the Philistine king, accepted the fugitives and gave David the town of Ziklag for a home. He did this, not so much out of friendship, but because they both had a common enemy in King Saul.

The day came when the Philistine armies were heading north to make war against Saul, King of Israel. David and his mighty men showed up volunteering to fight with them against Saul. The other Philistine lords were afraid that David would switch his allegiance in the midst of battle, so they sent David and his mighty men back to their home in Ziklag.

Upon returning to Ziklag, David found that the Amalekites had invaded the city, plundered its spoil, burned it to the ground, and taken their wives and children as hostages.

So, at Ziklag David and his faithful warriors lost everything they had, their wives, their children, their homes, and all their possessions! David's men were so disheartened and discouraged that they talked about killing David.

Defeated and desperate, David turned to God. In the midst of the chaos and crisis, we are told *"David encouraged himself in the Lord."* (1 Sam 30:6)

In the burned rubble of Ziklag, David "inquired of the Lord, saying, Shall I pursue after the troop? Shall I overtake them?" And God answered him, "Pursue; for thou shalt surely overtake them, and without fail, recover all." (1 Sam. 30:8)

We are told that David and his little band of 400 men pursued the Amalekites, surprised them, slaughtered them, and recovered all that had been taken away from them. He and his men got back their wives, their children, and all the possessions that had been taken from them.

In fact, they even recovered the spoils from the other cities that had been plundered, ending up with more than they started with.

That is the Biblical story of the city of Ziklag. Now I want you to see how God began to introduce our circumstances into its history.

## 2. Ziklag: A Place Of Leaning

On a sunny August day in 2011, I was called into my boss's office. I had served as Director of Education for this company for fifteen years. I loved my job that included a mixture of educating the community about financial literacy, plus counseling people who were already in financial trouble.

I had just been called into his office a week earlier and given "cudo's" for scoring high on a "phantom counselor call." These calls were made sporadically to make sure our counselors were offering quality counseling. I felt I had really good job security in that I had always received good reviews, and the education aspect of our business was vital to meeting IRS regulations for financial education.

My boss began, "Jim, you are going to be 62 years old in two months, you are not healthy, and you are costing my company a lot of money in insurance." He told me effective immediately I would no longer be regarded as an employee.

Then, he then advised me to sign up for Medicare and Social Security when I turned 62 and establish an LLC for tax purposes. And with that, my status as a fifteen-year valued employee was ended.

He then offered me the option of working for his business as an independent education contractor, doing exactly what I had been doing for 15 years, but with no benefits. I would receive a small "salary" per month and be paid for education work on a per item basis. But all my benefits as an employee would be gone.

He advised me to "sleep on it" and let him know what I wanted to do.

I left his office that warm, August afternoon, totally stunned. I think "numb" is a good description of how I felt. I spoke to no one and left for the day.

I was in shock. Getting terminated was absolutely the last thing on my mind. Because of my position as Director of Education, my colleagues had even joked that I would be last on the totem pole to ever be terminated. Our company needed my education programs to meet IRS approval to operate.

I called my wife and told her what had occurred. At first, she thought I was joking, but I assured her I was not. I shared with her I did not know how we were going to make it, losing my job just before I turned 62, especially since I wear an insulin pump and am uninsurable.

We both agreed that God would help us figure it all out, and that somehow He has a plan for our future.

I spoke to no one in the office and left early that warm Monday afternoon. During the drive home what had just happened began to hit me! I started thinking about the show I had watched on Animal Planet the night before.

It was a documentary about how lions hunt. They filmed a lion pride as they stalked a herd of wildebeest. They explained that the lions target any wildebeest that is old, sick, crippled, or weak. They showed how that animal is separated from the rest of the herd, isolated, and attacked. As the rest of the herd stands by, unable to help, the wildebeest is killed and devoured.

—

I felt like that had just happened to me. Everyone else in the office would return home to things being just as they had been the day before. But I would return home, having been fired after fifteen years of faithful service.

I felt absolutely alone. Fear gripped my heart and panic struck way down deep in my soul. Had I had really been targeted for "the kill" because I was in my early 60's, have diabetes, and wear an insulin pump? I had been separated from the herd, terminated, and now was faced with a scary, uncertain future.

A future that left me wondering how on earth we would survive on such a reduced income stream. I also wondered how I could ever afford my diabetic supplies without any health insurance.

As the hours passed that day, I was pretty much overtaken with fear and anger. How could I be discarded in such a manner as this? I had always gotten excellent reviews. I had implemented new and innovative education programs.

I thought this man, who claimed to be a Christian, was my friend. I thought I was valued.

Didn't he know how often I had prayed for him and his family? Didn't he know how often that I had prayed that God would help me make his business prosper?

That evening was awful! I received a phone call from my senior counselor and friend, who had been informed only that I would have my full attention turned on education matters, and not have to carry a counseling load too. He and I had talked occasionally about that possibility, and now he thought that the time had come for that to occur. He was happy for me.

—

That is, until I told him that all my employee benefits had been taken away, and my salary reduced to $1000 per month. He was furious! He promised to do whatever he could for me, and said he would pray for me to have wisdom to know how to handle it all.

As you might guess, sleep did not come that night. I went to my home office about 3AM and laid my head on my desk and wept. I opened my Bible and tried to pray, but I found that the words did not come. I finally told the Lord how angry I was. I told Him how afraid I was. I told Him that I was so upset inside, I could hardly think straight.

Ginny and I had both worked hard all our life, and carefully struggled to become debt free, and now it seemed that all that was for nothing!

I began to thumb through the Psalms. I read one of the Psalms where King David was sharing his fear and uncertainty as he fled from King Saul who sought to take his life.

I read Psalm 42:5, 8b *"Why art thou cast down, O my soul? And why art thou disquieted in me? Hope thou in God: for I shall yet praise him for the help of his countenance...in the night his song shall be with me and my prayer shall be unto the God of my life."*

There was a cross-reference in this verse that I followed to 1 Samuel 30:6, *"David encouraged himself in the Lord his God."*

This was my first introduction to the chapter that I was to learn was all about what happened at the city of Ziklag.

This verse "David encouraged himself in the Lord" was such a blessing to read that night. As I thought about it, God began to open my eyes and let me see that, in the midst of this crisis, I was trying to handle this situation on my own.

—

I had not allowed God to be brought into the equation. In my anger and hurt, I had totally forgotten the fact that He was still in control of things – including my future.

I prayed for God to do for me what he had done for David so many years ago. I asked for Him to be my encouragement and my hope for the future. I told Him I did not know how we would survive this situation, but I was willing to trust Him.

The peace that filled my heart was amazing. The anger left and an amazing calmness flooded my soul that was unexplainable. The circumstances had not changed, but God was changing something inside of me! He was encouraging me that everything would be okay.

What God had done for David, He was literally doing for me! He had given me an absolute peace about the situation. I had become the recipient of what the Apostle Paul referred to in the New Testament as *"the peace of God that passes all understanding."* (Phil. 4:7)

As I sat in my office that early morning, I remembered preaching through Philippians years ago when I was a pastor. I remember concluding that this "peace" that Paul referred to was the very same peace that Jesus talked about when he told his disciples, *"Peace I leave with you, my peace I give unto you."* (John 14:27)

It is the peace that God offers us in the midst of great turmoil and storm. It is the very peace that He Himself possesses by nature! It is not something He manufactures and gives to us, but instead a peace that comes from His presence - a quiet, calming, "it's going to be okay" peace.

I thought about the time Jesus was in the boat with His disciples and a storm hit. It must have been a really bad storm because His disciples were panicked, and some of them had

—

been professional fisherman. You recall they had to wake Jesus up to get Him to help them! Now, that's peace.

And I remember what Jesus said to the storm, *"Peace, be still."* He not only possessed peace, He was able to transfer that peace to the storm! The Greek language implies that the storm stopped immediately - right away. The waters did not slosh and eventually calm, they calmed instantly!

That's the kind of peace that Jesus Christ possesses, and that is the kind of peace He shared with me that night.

Wow! I had never in my life experienced such a soul saturating peace. Not like I did that night. But then, I don't believe I ever needed it like I needed it that night. The chaos was turned into calm, the storm into stillness, and the panic into peace. I had leaned hard on God and let Him enter the picture, and everything inside me changed.

I was at the very end of what I could do, and at that point, God began to do what only He could do.

This was my first introduction to 1 Samuel 30 and the events surrounding Ziklag. I could never had known then how many times God would lead me back to this passage or how precious the word "Ziklag" would become in my vocabulary.

As I write these words, years later, a genuine peace quiets my soul just to hear the word "Ziklag."

Ziklag is a Place of Leaning. It is the place where we bring God into the equation. It is the place where we are forced to "lean not to our own understanding" and instead, begin to lean on Him.

### 3. Ziklag: A Place Of Loss

**The Contract.** After my August 1st termination, I worked without a contract as an independent contractor for two months before my boss ended my relationship with his company. He had verbally outlined the education venues he wanted me to do, and the amounts I would be paid for each.

This new job would be exactly what I was already doing for the last 15 years, except I would receive no benefits and much less income. Still, it was the only option on the horizon.

Apparently, this decision to terminate me was rather sudden. I say this because there was no contract ready for me to sign that would detail our verbal agreements. In fact, the contract was not presented to me until seven weeks later!

I had persuaded my boss to postpone my actual "employee" termination date to October 1st, so I could have time to schedule education meetings and have a revenue stream "in the pipeline." Otherwise, I would have had no income at all for at least 6-8 weeks.

Within a few days, my boss began to change the verbal agreements we had reached in his office. He removed some of the educational venues all together and greatly devalued other venues from the amounts he, himself, had given to them originally.

When I contacted him and asked him about the changes he was making, he told me that our verbal agreements were "fluid" and not meant to be understood as unchangeable.

That's when I began to suspect that he was not being up front with me, and that he had an agenda to eventually get rid of me altogether.

So, I went to his office the next day and flatly asked him if he

—

were "setting up our arrangement to fail?" I remember his reply to my question, "Oh no, Jim, you are much too intelligent for me to try anything like that." At the time I could not tell if he were being serious or cynical.

I, then, strongly suggested that my contract be produced immediately so I could have the details of my working relationship in writing where they could not be altered.

Again, that contract was not presented to me until seven weeks later! By the time I had the contract, I had one week to read it, sign it, and return it in order to meet the October 1 employee termination deadline. I also had completed over $3000 of education work.

Around September 20th,he sent me a draft of the Independent Contractor Agreement. Strangely enough, he had failed to remove the cover letter his attorney had included when she emailed the draft contract to him.

The cover letter revealed that the attorney had apparently been instructed to include in the contract a section dealing with Intellectual Property. This would include the books I had written, the online education library, and the domains I owned for them. These were part of the other businesses I ran on the side while I worked for him fulltime.

The attorney was suggesting this Intellectual Property issue not be included in the contract because it was a separate issue and had nothing to do with my job description.

When the long-awaited contract came the next day, I saw my boss's true intention. He had inserted a section right in the middle where I was to agree to sign over ownership of all my Intellectual Property to him.

I referred to this in the Foreword, but will explain it a bit more

—

now.

This IP material included several books I had written under contract with a separate entity, an online financial education library, and website domains. Even though I owned the legal copyrights, he was determined that he was going to "win" the argument that he owned these materials.

He purchased nearly 7000 copies of one of my financial books as part of his IRS required financial education program. He also used (free of charge) my online financial library on each of his four company websites. He occasionally covered some of the maintenance costs of the online library and each year signed a tax receipt for my "donation" of the services to his non-profit business.

Here's what the long-awaited Independent Contractor Agreement revealed:

1. It stipulated that my contract would have to be reviewed in just ninety days.

**2.** It also stated that I could be terminated with a three-day notice for any reason! Remember, I would be doing the very same job that I had been doing for 15 years with high accolades.

3. It required that I sign over ownership of all my Intellectual Property to   Him.

4. It prohibited me from filing any type of discrimination lawsuit.

I could see the "handwriting on the wall."  After turning over to him ownership of all my IP materials, my job could have been over after the first 90 days, or I could be fired with just a three day notice. At that time I would not be able to file for

———

unemployment because I would not be an employee of the company. I also could not bring any legal action.

I had no other options before me other than to sign this agreement. I told a friend that I had been put "between a rock and a hard place."

The very next day I heard a song on the radio for the first time as I drove in the car. The name of the song is "The Rock's Between The Hard Place And You." I joked that God must have been "eavesdropping" on my conversation with my friend!

My suspicion was correct. This whole plan had indeed been orchestrated to "fail." I cannot tell you how much that hurt. In order to "win," he had set up this whole arrangement to get rid of me in the near future.

Within a couple of days, I called an attorney friend of mine to have lunch and get his advice. I laid out what had taken place as objectively as I could, and asked him if he thought I had legal ground to defend myself.

He said he thought that I did and gave me the name of a law firm that dealt only in discrimination cases. On September 2 Ginny and I met with an attorney and explained what had taken place. We were trying to be open to all of our options including legal intervention, but that option was at the very bottom of our list. We did not want to do that.

The attorney asked me if, after what had transpired in the preceding weeks, I thought my boss planned to keep me around in the future. I had to truthfully answer "No." She said that her firm accepts only one out of every twelve cases offered to them, but this would be one she would accept if we went forward.

---

We told her we needed time to consider what we would do and made no commitment that day.

**Another Visit to Ziklag.** That night I made my second visit to 1 Samuel 30 and the circumstances surrounding Ziklag.

As some of you know who have gone through times of great stress, sleep does not come easily. I tried to sleep but ended up going to my office to read and pray. We sincerely wanted to discern what God wanted us to do with all of this.

My heart was once again very fearful. I knew that I was not insurable and had been told that, at age 62, no one would train me for a different job. But if I did not sign the agreement, how would we make it financially? It was not a choice between a Plan A and a Plan B – there was only a Plan A here.

I turned once again to that passage in 1 Samuel 30 where I had read that *"David encouraged himself in the Lord"* (v.30) because I sought again the peace that God had given me that night back in August.

I studied the circumstances surrounding verse 30 and saw that this "encouragement" was given to David in a time of great loss. David had suffered the loss of his wife, children, home, city, and every possession he owned. It was all taken from him in one day! He was left with only "right now" – his future was devastated!

Imagine that! Every person he held dear, every possession he owned, and every prospect for a bright future was gone! This was not only true for David; it was true for each of his 600 mighty warriors!

God had personally promised David that he would sit on the Throne of Israel as King. How could that possibly come true?

—

And even if it did some day, what would it matter if he ruled alone having lost all the people he loved?

We are told in verse 4 that *"David and the people that were with him lifted up their voice and wept, until they had no more power to weep."* I thought to myself, "My situation is bad, but losing your job at age 62 is nothing compared to the loss that David suffered!"

Added to this, the next verse tells us that *"the people spoke of stoning him because the soul of the people was grieved, every man for his sons and his daughters."*

No family, no finances, no future, and no friends!

That's what I needed to understand about David's situation before I could begin to understand the real meaning of "David encouraged himself in the Lord."

It was David's unimaginable loss that led him to lean on the Lord and find encouragement. It was his great need that brought him to his great God! I thought of the words penned elsewhere by David, *"It is good for me that I have been afflicted, that I might learn thy statutes."* (Psalm 119:71)

I knew that. I had even preached on that subject before. I had even shared with folks along the way the words of the great Christian Pastor and author, A.W. Tozer, "I doubt that God can ever use a man greatly, until He has hurt him deeply."

But we had not suffered any great losses for some time now. I had not had to make a visit to Ziklag, The Place of Loss, for some time. I had no reason to see how much God could help me, because I lived in a cycle of comparable peace and prosperity. Sort of like traveling down the road of life on "cruise control."

Leaning on God like I had to now was simply not necessary before, because there was no great loss.

Could it be that the deeper things we will learn about God are learned in the midst of problems and storms?

I am not sure how it all works together, but I am beginning to think that one of the valuable benefits of suffering loss is that the loss forces one to lean on God.
I began to understand that night how God intended the loss of my job to be the beginning of a new level of leaning on Him.

I also began to realize that Ziklag was able to teach its lessons because it was a Place of Loss. It is the hurting and the heartache that were bringing me to a point of hearing; hearing what God wanted to say to me.

A few days later I took my third journey to Ziklag and learned another valuable lesson about it - it is also a place of Leading.


## 4. Ziklag: A Place Of Leading

On the heels of David's great loss, he asked God what his next step should be *"Shall I pursue after this troop? Shall I overtake them?"*

Frankly, a more ludicrous question has never been asked! David had at the most 600 men in his army. The Amalekites had several thousand! Why would David even entertain the thought that he could somehow affect the outcome of what had happened? Did he think that his 600 soldiers could actually stand up to the thousands in the Amalekites' army?

How could he possibly believe he could do anything to change the outcome of what had occurred? One would envision God laughing at such a question as his!

---

But remember that this man, David, was the little guy who years before had been sent by God to stand before the great giant, Goliath.

David had heard Goliath boldly defy the army of Israel and Israel's God and went before King Saul and said, "You have no reason to fear this big goon! I will go slay him for you. God will help me kill him just as He helped me slay the lion and the bear."

Goliath was a giant from Gath who stood 9 feet 9 inches tall, wore a 125-pound breastplate, and carried a spear whose head alone weighed 15 pounds!

It was to this great hulk of a warrior that this same David had said years before, *"I come to thee in the name of the Lord of hosts, the God of the armies of Israel, whom thou hast defiled. This day will the Lord deliver thee into mine hand; and I will take thine head from thee…that all the earth may know that there is a God in Israel, And all the assembly shall know that the Lord saveth not with sword and spear; for the battle is the Lord's, and He will give you into our hands."* (1 Samuel 17:45-47)

That's why David was now asking God if he should pursue after the Amalekites – he knew that the battle would not be won by the strength of his army! It could only be won by the strength of His God!

He knew that God often uses little things, weak things, seemingly insignificant things to do great things! He did not need to know how God would bring the victory; all He needed to know was what God wanted him to do.

David was ready to do his part, and let God do His part. His was not to understand it all – his part was just to trust God to keep His word!

—

Here's God's answer to David: *"Pursue; for thou shalt surely overtake them, and without fail recover all."* 1 Samuel 30: Here's an answer that appears to be pretty easy to understand.

David asked, *"Shall I pursue?"*

God answered, *"Pursue."*

I too, genuinely wanted to know what God wanted me to do for the next step. Should I pursue a legal action against my former boss? In all sincerity I asked the Lord to be crystal clear in His answer to me.

When I read David's question, *"Shall I pursue?"* I saw it as the same question that I was asking.

And when God clearly answered David, *"Pursue"* He was answering me too. I asked Him for a clear answer and here it was - "Pursue."

Just a few weeks earlier the attorney told me that I had a solid case, but I just did not feel at that time that I should pursue it.

But now I saw what my boss's intent was, and I knew that my prospect of working for him in any capacity could not come about. I also knew that God had given me direction in answer to my prayer. I was to "Pursue."

On September 27th, my boss sent me a Severance letter in which he withdrew the offer to work as an independent contractor. He said he thought it would be best for everyone if we ended our relationship all together. He also said how much he appreciated all my years of service. You are correct; I did find that a bit hard to believe.

I, frankly, was amazed at the stipulations in his Severance letter! In order to receive payment for the $3000+ education

———

invoice I had submitted for August/September, and in order to receive one month's severance pay, I was required to:

**1.** Sign over ownership of all my intellectual property to him.
**2.** Promise that I would never tell anything I knew that would make the company look bad in the eyes of the public.
**3.** Promise that I would not pursue any discrimination lawsuit or any other retaliatory action.

Under those terms, I could not sign the Severance Agreement, So, I left the company for which I had worked for 15 years with absolutely nothing. I was even refused reimbursement for the eleven days of vacation time that I still had coming to me. They told me that "unused" vacation time is not reimbursed.

Within a few short days, they began an attack of legal threats and harassments that lasted for months until I hired an expensive attorney and threatened a law suit for harassment.

Now as I read David's question and God's answer, I knew down deep in my heart that God had led me to this passage in 1 Samuel 30. Here was His direction for the next step I should take – *"Pursue...and without fail recover all."*

Frankly, I did not know what God meant by the phrase *"and without fail recover all."* I did not know if this meant God would return to me all the lost wages, or if I would come out ahead financially, or if it meant the benefits I would gain spiritually, would outweigh the losses. I just did not know.

I did not know what that phrase meant, but I did know what we were to do for the next step – "Pursue."

I did not know how this all would end. I did not know if the Civil Rights Commission would approve our case, or if it would ever come to trial. God only told me what I needed to

——

do for the next step, and asked me to leave the rest to Him. My job was to trust Him. His job was to bring about His plan and purpose in His own way.

That leads me to share something with you about the will of God. The best way to know the will of God is to be in His will right now. If we are where He wants us to be, doing what He wants us to do, He will find a way to communicate with us as to the next step.

Understand again, I was not looking for God to validate my desire to go to court. I sincerely wanted to know if this was the course He had for me, but it was not something either of us wanted to do. Unless I was sure of His leading, I would never have pursued court action.

Here, in this passage about David's experience at Ziklag, was God's answer to me. Couched in the events of Ziklag, my question was asked and the answer was given!

I understand that God could lead His children in a variety of ways, but I have always looked to the Bible as the main method of His leading for me. Once I see His will revealed in His Word, I can rest my whole weight on it. It is not based on emotion or a feeling, but instead, the Holy Spirit revealing God's will in the pages of God's Word.

In fact, during this time of great turmoil and stress there were numerous other passages that God gave me that demonstrated that God knew what was happening in our lives and was planning on using these events to accomplish some plan He had for us.

These were promises that were so real to me, they gave me comfort, and solace, and peace. Here are some of those promises:

—

*"When you lie down, you will not be afraid: when you lie down, your sleep will be sweet. Have no fear of sudden disaster or of the ruin that overtakes the wicked, for the Lord will be your confidence and will keep your foot from being snared."* Proverbs 3:24-26

*"They repay me evil for good and hatred for my friendship. Appoint an evil man to oppose him, let an accuser stand at his right hand, when he is tried, let him be found guilty...Let them know that it is your hand, that You, O Lord, have done it"* Psalm 109:5-7, 27

*"Proud men have hidden a snare for me; they have spread out the cords of their nets and have set their traps for me along my path. O Sovereign Lord, my strong deliverer, who shields my head in the day of battle – do not grant the wicked their desires, O Lord; do not let their plans succeed, or they will become proud. Let the heads of those who surround me be covered with the trouble their lips have caused."* Psalm 140:5, 7-9

*"But the Lord your God will deliver them over to you, throwing them into great confusion until they are destroyed."* Deuteronomy 7:23

*"He who digs a hole and scoops it out falls into the pit he has made. The trouble he causes recoils on himself, his violence comes down on his own head."* Psalm 7:15

*"I will praise the Lord, who counsels me; even at night my heart instructs me. I have set the Lord always before me. Because He is at my right hand, I will not be shaken."* Psalm 16:7-8

*"He reached down from on high and took hold of me, he drew me out of deep waters. He rescued me from my powerful enemy, from my foes, who were too strong for me. They confronted me in the day of my disaster, but the Lord was my support. He brought me out into a spacious place; he rescued me because he delighted in me."* Psalm 18:16-19

—

There were literally dozens of others verses that God shared with me to promise me that He was right by my side. In fact there were so many promises that I began to wonder again if I were guilty of going to Scripture and making it say what I wanted it to say, not what God was really saying.

I prayed, "God, I really want to know what you want me to do. I cannot handle this on my own. I need your strength, and power, and wisdom to make it through this time. Please lead me to verses where I can clearly hear Your voice and know your will."

The next day I read this verse: *"The Lord confides in those who fear Him"* (Psalm 25:14). I had been asking God for guidance, and He had been giving me all these wonderful promises – why on earth would I question whether or not they are coming from Him? That *is* how He communicates to His children – through His Word!

After that, I quit doubting whether the verses that God was giving me were actually promises from Him. Of course they were. They were the answers to my prayers.

You recall it was David, the same guy who was at Ziklag that penned these words, *"Thy word is a lamp unto my feet and a light unto my path."* Psalm 119:105. That is the basic method by which God communicates to His children.

A person who has never come into a personal relationship with God through Jesus Christ, would no doubt find this thinking hard to grasp. But remember Jesus told His disciples, *"My sheep hear my voice, and I know them, and they follow me."* (John 10:27)

We do not hear God's voice through fiery letters written in the sky, or through telegrams delivered by angels. We hear God's voice as He speaks to us through His Word.

———

I have to tell you, I related to David's inability to bring about the fulfillment of God's promise. He only had 600 men to battle the Amalekites and get all his possessions back! I had no wisdom, no resources, and very little energy to get involved in a court case about age discrimination.

But that is exactly what I felt God was leading me to do! And He primarily used the circumstances surrounding Ziklag to reveal His will very clearly to me.

The next day, I shared with my wife what I had read.
Although we were still both apprehensive, we decided to make another appointment with the discrimination attorney to take a hard look at our options.

It was simply amazing that, after the meeting with her, we both were absolutely convinced that this was the will of God for us.

We immediately filed an Age Discrimination claim with the Civil Rights Commission. That commission weighs the evidence and must concur that there is a solid case before one can proceed in court. Within a few weeks, they agreed that I had a solid case and we began preparation for trial.
In the weeks following my job loss, Ziklag, This Place of Long Ago (1000 BC), had become to me:

* A Place of **Leaning** – *"David encouraged himself in the Lord"* (1 Samuel 30:6)
* A Place of **Loss** – *"it was burned with fire; and their wives and their son were taken captive…they lifted up their voice and wept, until they had no more power to weep"* (1 Samuel 30:3-4)
* A Place of **Leading** – *"Shall I pursue?...Pursue, for thou shalt surely overtake them and without fail, recover all."* (1 Samuel 30:8).

## 5. Ziklag: A Place Of Love

That may sound really strange at first. How did Ziklag become a place of Love? That is an amazing story! It became that for David, and it became that to us.

It is interesting that as we suffer loss, our faith, our trust, and our love for God can increase. The loss, and the resulting dependence upon God, gives us a much better vantage point to experientially know Who God is and what He can do.

Every time my heart would become fearful, God would do something to remind me how very much He loved me. He would bring about circumstances that would bring me back to the place where I remembered that this was all about Him, and not just me. He was the One who was in control of my life and my future, and He was the One who was behind the scenes of this crisis working things out in such a way so His plan and His purposes would be accomplished.

In the months following the October 1, 2011, termination I tried to figure out how to bring in an income. I signed up for Social Security at age 62, which gave us a constant income flow. It also limited the amount of money I could earn on a W-2. This prompted me to form a Limited Liability Corporation, which would better serve me for tax purposes.

To help me think clearly, I compiled a number of articles about job loss for my online financial library. It was very helpful to me to educate myself with this information, and then be able to share it with others. I learned principles that helped me, and therefore, would help others in a similar situation of job loss.

For now, I will not go into more detail about those days, because I want to stay focused on how God used Ziklag to show me just how very much He loves me.

———

1 Samuel 30 and Ziklag were beginning to take on meaning for me. It was there that God taught me how to "encourage" myself in Him. It was there that I was directed to "pursue" my former employer and file a discrimination lawsuit. And it was there that God promised me I would *"recover everything that had been taken from me"* (whatever that meant). Certainly "Ziklag" had become a household word. Each time I heard it, I was reminded of God's love for me.

# Part Two

*How Many Times
Does God Have
To Tell Me?*

God not only led me to this passage multiple times in the first days and weeks, but in an almost miraculous way, continued to lead me back to 1 Samuel 30. Just when I needed to remember what God had promised me, a reminder about Ziklag would appear.

It frankly is somewhat humbling to have to admit to you how many times God told me the same thing. I began to feel like the disciples when Jesus asked them, *"Are you still so dull?"* (Matthew 15:16)

You would think that when God tells us something, one time would be enough, but my old callous heart has a tendency to forget so quickly. It seems that each time my heart would become fearful, and I would need reassurance, God would do something to remind me of Ziklag and the promises He made to me from 1 Samuel 30.

Let me show you what I mean.

### Reminder 1: Is That Guy Talking To Me?

In April 2012 I was spending the night in a Motel 6 on the western edge of Iowa. I had conducted a Smart Discipline for Parents Seminar that evening in a local school and decided not to drive home that night. I had gone to sleep at the wheel a couple of years before, and totaled my Jeep. So, spending the night occasionally seemed a better option.

As the night hours lingered, I simply could not get to sleep. I had communicated with my attorney the day before, and the details of the upcoming court case were on my mind. The more I tried to quit thinking about them, the more they persisted.

I have to confess, even though a great peace had flood my heart back in October as I applied the circumstances surrounding Ziklag to me, there were times when that peace

———

would be gone and fear be left instead.

I shut off the lights, turned my sleep sound machine to "loud," and laid in the dark trying to fall asleep. After several hours, I clicked the TV back on around 2 am, and there on the TV was one of those TV Preacher's pointing his finger at the camera.

I heard him say, "Listen to me and I will to tell you how God is going to return to you everything that was taken away!"

I smiled because I thought that statement surely applied to me having lost my job, my security, and maybe my future. That phrasing sounded so similar to what I had read months ago in 1 Samuel, it really caught my attention.

Then this TV Preacher proceeded to preach the first and only message I had ever heard on the events surrounding the City of Ziklag! I thought, "This is really weird! I had never heard about Ziklag before God used it in the wee hours of the morning right after I lost my job! Could it possible be that He was now using this TV preacher to remind me of those promises He had given me months ago?"

I sat up in the bed to listen to this preacher expound the story of David's great loss and how God promised him that He would return everything that had been taken from Him.

I knew without a doubt that this was not a coincidence. God in His great love for me had used this very unusual situation to focus my mind once again on the promises He had given me before.

I whispered, "Thank you Lord. I know that message was for me. You wanted to remind me that your peace depends on my trusting your promise! Thank you for going out of Your way to remind me how much you love me."

———

With that, I flicked off the lights, turned my sleep sound machine volume back up, and went to sleep.

## *Reminder 2: The Next Passage To Read*

The next morning I arose, showered, and went to the "kitchen" for the continental breakfast that came with my stay. I went back to the room and decided that I had plenty of time to read a bit out of the Bible I had packed in my suitcase.

I have always preferred to read through Bible books systematically instead of jumping from passage to passage. I often combine something from the Old Testament with something from the New Testament.

I have also tried to follow the advice of the old Black preacher who said, "You needs to reads the Bible until you comes to a verse that you can rest your whole weight upon!" That method would be the opposite of just reading the Bible to fulfill the requirements of some Bible reading schedule. The goal, of course, is to read until you get something out of what you are reading."

So, I opened the Bible to where the Bible markers were stuck, first the New Testament passage, then Old Testament passage. I was simply amazed to see that the next Old Testament passage I was to read was 1 Samuel 30. Remember that's the one about Ziklag!

With great interest I read again all that God has shared with me back in the fall. David's question and God's answer were still there just like they were before – and I was assured that they were there for me!

The night before a TV preacher preaches on the very passage that I was destined to read the next morning, and that is the passage I was led to that replaced my fear with God's great peace.

I cannot express to you how much I felt loved by God that morning in that little motel room in Western Iowa. It was either a couple of really neat coincidences, or there was a God in Heaven who was just close as to me as close could be!

I called my wife on the trip home and told her what had happened. I told her how I was assured that we were in the place we needed to be, doing the things we need to do in order to let God do what He wanted to do.

## Reminder 3: Who's Singing That Song?

Fast forward to Wednesday, May 23, 2012. I was at my bathroom sink brushing my teeth with my battery-powered toothbrush. I knew that my task that morning was to focus on a lengthy questionnaire that my attorney had asked me to fill out.

I had turned on the TV in the bedroom and was playing the channel that featured only Christian music. In fact, it featured only Southern Gospel music, my favorite.

I remember hearing the music in the background as I "brushed away," when I thought I heard the singer say something like "Gather 'round children and listen to me. I am going to tell you how God is going to return everything that was taken away from you."

What? I turned the toothbrush off, hit the information button on the TV remote, and saw that this song was by some group from the 1950's called "The Sensational Nightingales."

You want to know what the name of their song was? "I'm Takin' Back What The Devil Stole From Me." You want to know what their song was about? It was all about 1 Samuel 30

—

and the story of Ziklag. It details how God returned to David all that was taken away from him! Here's the address for them singing this song"http://youtu.be/I5eG6zbRujg."

Here's a group of singers I had never heard about, singing a song I had never heard, recorded clear back in the 1950's, all about a situation I was becoming more and more familiar with – Ziklag!

By then, I was getting used to the habit of talking out loud to God I guess, because I laughed out loud once again and said "I got the message, Lord! I will quit being fearful and trust the promises you gave me before!"

You tell me, dear friend, you think it was coincidental that a song recorded 60 years earlier about an obscure event in history – Ziklag - just happened to be playing at the time I was brushing my teeth with the TV on in the next room?

Stop to think about all the things that had to happen for me to hear that song at that time that morning:

**1.** Someone had to be familiar with the events of 1 Samuel 30 and Ziklag in order to write a song about it.
**2.** Someone had to be inspired to write the song.
**3.** Doors had to open so the song could make it into the market place.
**4.** A radio DJ had to be led to pull out that old song, play it on that specific morning right at the very time I was brushing my teeth.
**5.** I had to rise, eat, shower, all on cue or I would not have been brushing my teeth at that moment. Three minutes off in any direction and I would have missed hearing it!

I believe that God did all that so I could hear that 60-year-old song and have the peace of God flood my soul once again!

———

I was beginning to believe that God was going to great lengths to communicate His love and His leading to me!

Three times now I had been directed back to the passage that had given me such a sense of God's presence and peace. But God was not done yet!

On Sunday afternoon, July 22, 2012, I was sitting in our living room flipping through the TV channels. Us men have gotten extremely good at going through the TV channels quickly, ascertaining immediately if the channel is worth stopping to watch.

### Reminder 4: "My Sermon Today Is ... "

I am not sure what the channel was, but as I breezed by it I heard the word "Ziklag!" What? I could not believe my ears! Was somebody really talking about Ziklag – again?

That, dear friend, was exactly what was happening! TD Jakes, that great black preacher of the Potter's House was preaching! And what was the topic of his message that Sunday afternoon? It was none other than "The Crown Comes To Ziklag" from 1 Samuel 30!

Yes sir – there he was talking about how God returned to David everything that had been taken away from him. He went into detail explaining with the skill of a surgeon, how it is at those times of great loss that God will use the crisis to prepare us to wear a crown. You see, just after everything was returned to David, he was crowned King of the northern 10tribes of Israel. Now he was king over the entire nation, and would be for the next 40 years!

I called to my wife in the other room and said, "What would you guess TD Jakes is preaching on this afternoon?"

She said, "Don't tell me. Ziklag?"

—

That is four times since our first encounter with Ziklag that God was using some unusual circumstances to draw my attention back to the promises He gave me in the fall of 2011.

## Reminder 5: An 1850's Message For Today

I am not sure just who the source of this next reminder about Ziklag was, but it came in the form of a devotional from a great English preacher I admire, Charles Haddon Spurgeon.

Spurgeon was an English preacher in London from the 1820's to the 1860's. He is respectfully called "The Prince of Preachers" and is known for his eloquent, yet soul-stirring writings (he has more sermons in print than any other person in history).

So, I open the devotional that was attached to his email, and here is a sermon preached in August of 1850, from the pulpit of the Metropolitan Tabernacle in London, by CH Spurgeon.

What would you guess the topic of that 163-year-old sermon was? Yep – it was about ZIKLAG! I could not believe my eyes! I spent some time wiping tears from my eyes that morning!

Once again, God knew that I needed to be reminded of His great promises. He wanted me to remember that He was right by my side, fully aware of all that was happening in our lives. He wanted me to remember that all He was asking me to do was to trust Him.

For months, I received no further reminders about Ziklag, although there were times when I would go back to 1 Samuel and read the account again. It would always fill my heart with peace, and remind me how much God loved me. After all, He had reminded me of this passage five times over the last year!

—

## Reminder 6: Another TV Preacher

I am writing right now in February 2013. Our trial has not taken place yet. In fact I just received a call a couple of days ago that the court date has finally been set – December 9, 2013! That's over two years from the time I was terminated from my job!

With the call about the setting of the court date, I was told that I am required to give my "deposition" to the opposing attorney in April. I was advised to go over my notes very thoroughly to remind myself of the events that had taken place.

The night of the call I went to bed a bit earlier than my wife. That is not uncommon for us. I have back problems, and watching the TV from the bed is a more comfortable position for me.

I am flipping through the channels (as usual) when I hear someone say "Ziklag!"

I stop flipping and go back that station. There is another TV preacher speaking to his TV audience. He says, "My burden tonight is to tell you how God is going to return to you everything that the devil took from you." Then he proceeded to share the story about David at Ziklag from 1 Samuel 30. He told how God did a work there that left doubt in no one's thinking that it was God winning the battle, not David.

I yelled into the next room to my wife, "Can you step around the corner just a minute?"

She stuck her head in the room and I asked, "What do you suppose this guy's preaching on tonight?"

She said, "Tell me no more – it has to be Ziklag!" It was!

—

*Reminder 7: "My Pastor just preached about that!"*
In April 2013, I was invited to the Council Bluffs, IA, area to speak to a number of high schools about financial literacy. Now, that does not sound like a trip that would have anything to do with the Bible, does it?

I was pleasantly surprised to discover the young man from the bank that had invited me was a believer, and in fact, had been a youth pastor for six years. As he drove me from place to place, we really had a neat time of talking about the Lord.

On one of the longer drives I shared with him how God had so clearly provided His leadership to me by sending me to 1 Samuel 30. I shared with him about Ziklag and was very surprised to see that he appeared to be familiar with the events of that chapter.

I said to him, "You seem to be very familiar with the circumstances surrounding Ziklag. How on earth do you know about it? It is kind of hidden away in the Old Testament."

He responded, "Oh, that's because my Pastor just preached on it last Sunday. He talked about that phrase "David encouraged himself in the Lord," and told us all about what happened at Ziklag."

For a few minutes I was speechless. What would the mathematical probability of his pastor preaching about Ziklag be the Sunday before he drives me around in his car on Monday? Amazing.

## Reminder 8: "You're on the right track!"
This reminder came in July of 2013. It had been a couple of months since I had added any more information to these collections of thoughts. I was at a standstill, and was not sure

just which direction to go in sharing the events of the last couple of years with you.

Then Sunday morning, July 14th came. While I was taking a shower, the direction God wanted me to take in my writings started to take shape, so I hurried up and finished my shower so I could find a piece of paper and write down the outline.

That afternoon I went to my computer and began typing my thoughts at the place where I had been "stuck" for months. I am not a good typist, and I had a hard time typing as fast as my mind was working.

I paused for a minute to thank God for giving me direction to continue writing this information to you. In the other room, Ginny was doing a crossword while listening to music in the background on television.

And that's when I heard the same song I had heard a year ago on May 23, 2012, while brushing my teeth – The Sensational Nightingales from the 1950's once again singing "I'm Takin' It Back!"

That is definitely not one of the regular songs that station plays. It is the only song I have ever heard that is taken from 1 Samuel 30 concerning the account of King David losing everything at Ziklag, and God promising that he would *"recover all."*

Hearing that song at that time was like God saying to me, "You are back writing what I want you to write. I am still right beside you giving you direction and wisdom."

What an encouragement to see God giving another reminder to us, that our responsibility is simply to trust Him and let Him work out the details to life's problems. It was a lesson that He was trying to teach us – His ability begins at the point

—

where our ability ends.

I thought of the phrase I had heard as a Bible college freshman, "God is not looking for your ability; He is looking for your availability."

### *Reminder 9: Just taking a walk...*

Just like the times before, the ninth reminder came quite unexpectedly as Ginny and I was taking a walk together on Sunday night, August 11, 2013. We had just rounded the curve and were starting to head back home when the mother of two new piano students came driving down the road toward us.

She knew that Ginny was a Christian and for some reason started telling us about the great message she had heard at church that morning.

"My preacher was preaching about the time that King David..."

And we knew instinctively what she was going to say."...about the time King David suffered a horrible loss because the Amalakites burned his city and took all of his family and things away."

Ginny said, "That was when he was at Ziklag."

"Yea, that was it, Ziklag!" And she proceeded to tell us in great detail how God promised David that He would return everything that was taken from him!"

After she finished, I shared with her how I had been fired two years earlier for being old, sick, and too expensive for their insurance. I told her that God had promised me shortly after I lost my job that He was going to return everything that had been taken from us. I told her that God had done so from 1 Samuel 30 and the story of Ziklag.

———

I told her that she had just been used of the Lord to be the 9th Reminder about Ziklag. She said she had never heard the name Ziklag" before that morning and agreed that this seemed like more than a coincidence.

She paused a minute and then asked us if we went to the Evangelical Free Church in Ankeny. I told her that we used to. She said a couple of years back she had received their prayer list, and that my job loss was one of the items listed for prayer. She told us that she had prayed for me by name about that loss because it seemed so unfair to get fired like that.

What an encouragement to "coincidentally" run into someone whom I had never met before, who had prayed for me by name about my job loss, then shared with me once again the story about David and Ziklag.

She then asked if she could pray for us, that God would make His promises come about, and that He would give us faith to just trust Him.

As she pulled away, Ginny and I laughed out loud. Again, we knew what the "holy laughter" of Abraham was all about. God told him at age 75 that Sarah, his wife, would have a child in her old age, and Abraham laughed out loud.

Abraham's laughter was not one of disrespect, but instead was a laugh of bewildering faith. His laughter said in essence, "Isn't that just like God to wait until it is impossible for us to have children, and then give us a child!" And at age 100 Abraham was given a son through Sarah, and his name was Isaac.

Every time I think that God is done with these precious "reminders," He gives us another one in a different way! Nine times now, over the course of one year, God led me back to 1 Samuel 30 to promise me that He was going to "return

—

everything that had been taken away from me." He used His Word, a late-night TV preacher, a 1950's Gospel singing group's song, a Sunday afternoon message by TD Jakes, an 1850 devotional by Charles Hadden Spurgeon, another TV preacher, a young man who had just heard his Pastor preach on 1 Samuel 30 the Sunday before, the same "I'm takin' It Back" song from the Sensational Nightingales a year later, and then the mother of a new piano student driving up the street while we are "just taking a walk."

Why did God feel it was necessary to give me these nine "reminders" about Ziklag? I really do not know, but they seem to come at just the right times. With me, those "fiery darts of doubt" seem to hit their "bulls-eye" so often, and my faith needs to be reinforced constantly.

The name of the city, Ziklag, will forever be embedded in my mind for as long as I live. Every time I hear it, I will reflect on the events that began in 2011, and how God went out His way to let me know everything would be all right.

My point in sharing this story with you is to let you know – not that I am someone special - but that we have a God Who loves us in a special way! He is so concerned about our troubled heart that He will go over-board to show us repeatedly what He is promising us. If we need to be reminded about the same thing nine times, God will remind us nine times. Whatever it takes to teach us that faith in His promises will replace fear.

God is able to be to us all that we need. It is not usually until we are in that place where God is all we have that we are able to see that He is all we need.

---

# Part Three

*The Bottom Drops Out Of Life!*

## The Phone Call

The timeline we have traveled thus far is from August 1, 2011, through the spring of 2013. I have intentionally tried to keep our focus on the things surrounding Ziklag.

Up to now 1 Samuel 30 was viewed only in its relationship to losing my job at age 62. Now as we continue, you will see how God's promises to me that "without fail" I will "recover all" had more application than just that of going to trial after losing my job.

It was Thursday morning, May 24th, 2012 around 8:45am. Ginny had left to teach piano lessons. She travels to their homes to teach, making it convenient for the families of her students.

About 9:10AM I heard the door open and Ginny entered with her cell phone up to her ear. Her face was white as snow. The call was from the wife of our 34-year -old Army son, Shawn.

Shawn was Ginny's youngest boy. He was already gone from home when we married, so we never really enjoyed a father-son type of relationship. It was always good, but never real close. At least it was not like the relationship that he had with his mom.

He had been deployed four times overseas during his seventeen-year career. He was now living near Ft. Rucker, AL, with his wife and four kids. He was serving as a helicopter pilot instructor and in August would be deployed a fifth time - to Honduras. He only had two more years to reach twenty years of service, and he could retire from the Army.

Shawn had committed suicide.

Four years earlier he had been sent home early from Afghanistan. The stress of being a "search and rescue" helicopter pilot had taken its toll on him. He was placed in a hospital Stateside. Ginny had flown to visit him, but was allowed to see him for only one half hour during her entire visit.

Since then he had been under a doctor's care, suffering from PTSD (Post Traumatic Stress Disorder). From all the official reports we have read afterward, there was no indication that he was suicidal. It came, as it often does, as a complete surprise to everyone who knew him.

The next 12 hours were the most excruciating, pain-filled hours that I have ever lived. I watched my precious wife call each of her remaining 5 children and tell them the awful news. She would break down into periods of great sobbing as she told them and then tried to comfort each of them the best she could.

By late afternoon, the migraine headache that Ginny had the previous day had returned, and she went to bed early in the evening. I heard her up several times during the night, and when I rose early the next morning, she was sitting with her Bible weeping.

The next day we made plans to drive to Ozark, Alabama, where Shawn had lived. This was a 20-hour drive, but we thought driving would give us more flexibility once we arrived, plus plane tickets were very expensive. We planned to leave Saturday and arrive there sometime Sunday afternoon. Funeral plans had not been made yet, but we were guessing the funeral would be mid-week.

### *"God-Hugs"*

On the trip down to Alabama we began to notice that God continued to do things for us that were a bit extraordinary. I guess the extraordinary need required an extraordinary

---

blessing. I've started calling these extraordinary blessings "God-hugs." I know that a man by the name of Squire Rushnell coined the phrase "God winks," so I will give him credit for the idea, but I prefer to call these happenings "God-hugs."

A God-hug is something that God does for His child while he is in the midst of severe crisis and need. It is something unusual and somewhat out of the ordinary. Some would call it a coincidence, but because of its very personal nature, you see it as a message from God to you.

With a God-hug, God is going the extra mile to make sure you understand how close He is and how much He cares.

A God-hug sends this message: "My child, I am fully aware of what you are going through, and I am right here beside you. I love you and invite you to climb up into my lap where I will put my arms around you and keep you safe."

A "God-hug" is portrayed for me in visual form through a picture I came across years ago. I do not know the artist. The stress of the pastorate had taken its toll on me, and I was on the verge of giving up and quitting.

I often prayed, "God, let me climb up into your lap and feel Your arms around me."

Then I came across a picture by Kathryn Brown that conveyed my sentiments exactly. I pasted a copy of it in the cover of my Bible and looked at it daily. It has remained there for more than 20 years. (http://www.jesusandthelamb.com/)

———

The God-hugs Ginny and I experienced conveyed the same message that this picture did to me so many years before. I have added the picture so you could see it.

As I continue sharing events in the next pages, I want to especially point out the God-hugs we received. My goal is to share with you, again, how much effort God exerts to assure us and remind us He is right beside us in the midst of difficulty.

—

## The Trip To Alabama

*God-hug 1: The Couple.* We left our home really early Saturday morning, got to St. Louis by late morning, and decided to stop and have lunch at a Culver's restaurant.

As I opened the door for Ginny, another lady spoke to her on the way into the restaurant, "I see you have out of town plates like we do. Are you on vacation down here?"

My wife said, "No." Then with hesitation, "We are on our way to our son's funeral. He was in the Army."

The lady was so compassionate to us, telling us that she too had lost a son who was in the military.

She asked if our son was killed in action. We said that he suffered from PTSD and had committed suicide after four tours of duty.

I do not remember the entire conversation with this lady and her husband, but I do remember that she told us she served on some national board of parents whose children had committed suicide. Her husband had served the last 17 years as a military officer in charge of distributing benefits to soldier's families who had died in active duty.

They were both Christian people who loved the Lord and instantly identified with the pain that engulfed us. We did not need to explain – they just understood.

Just before they left the restaurant she told us that the reason she had met us at the door was because she had gone back out to her car to get some sweetener for her drink. Both couples marveled that God was able to work out the timing exactly to have us meet so they could minister to us.

She handed me a note with their names and contact

---

information on it and at the bottom of the note she had written her deceased son's name. It was Shawn too.

It was not a big thing, but that meeting served to remind us that God was near. He was asking us to go through a really hard situation, but He was not going to abandon us. He was right beside us.

*God-hug 2: Locked Out.* Neither of us felt well that day. I am diabetic and wear an insulin pump, and Ginny was simply worn to a frazzle. We made frequent stops for bathroom breaks and tried to stay awake to drive.

At one such stop, Ginny had to wait to get into the women's room, then she was in there for quite a while. I guess the time seemed longer to me than normal, because she had slipped the car keys into her purse and, of course, taken her purse into the restroom with her.

I, therefore, was forced to stand outside our car that was parked in front of one of the pumps. It was locked. The place was so busy, cars were backed up behind each pump, especially ours, so I proceeded to tell those in my line that I could not move my car.

As I stood there in the heat for almost 45 minutes, an old guy in a pick up drove up to the pump next to me. As he pumped his gas, he told me that he and his grandson had traveled together to hear some Gospel bluegrass singers. He saw my license plate and asked me if I lived around there.

I told him no, and that we were headed to southern Alabama to attend our Army son's funeral. As we talked, I revealed that he suffered from PTSD and had just committed suicide.

The man quit pumping his gas and said to me, "Me and my

grandson are believers. God must have wanted us to stop here and meet you so we could pray for you." And right there in the gas station lot, next to the pumps, he prayed a simple prayer that God would wrap His arms around us and hold us close.

Most of the long trip is just a blur, but I remember we listened to Christian music, and the words ministered to our hearts in such a sweet way. It seemed that just the right words were being sung at just the right time to remind us of the promises we had from God. Ginny would be okay for a while, then she would break down into heaving sobs. I have never seen anyone cry as hard as she did.

*God-hug 3: The Father and Son.* Another of God's reminders took place at an IHOP about half way through Alabama. Ginny was a bit embarrassed to go inside to eat because her eyes were so swollen from crying. But we were hungry and thought the break would be good for us, so we pulled into the IHOP restaurant.

We were seated that Sunday noon in an area of the restaurant that was really crowded. The people at the tables near us were almost sitting in our laps.

After we ordered, Ginny began to weep. Her tears came so often and without any warning. It was as though her emotions had been blasted with a bomb. She could not control the tears or keep them from coming.

The couples on both sides of us tried to act like they did not see her, but I knew they did. Eventually, I felt it best to apologize to the people next to us. I explained that we were on the way to our Army son's funeral.

I will never forget the two men to the right of us. They were big rugged guys, a father and his adult son. I think a proper description of them would be "big rednecks."

I could see the father better because he was facing me. I noticed he got big tears in his eyes. As they stood to leave, he leaned over and quietly said to us, "My son and I are both Christians. We are so sorry for your loss. Would it be ok if I prayed for you?"

He stood next to us in that crowded restaurant with his big hand on my shoulder and prayed. It was as if God "showed up" in that room. As he prayed, the presence of God was so very real. We were dreading every mile we came closer to our destination. And when things seemed almost unbearable, God sent a father and his son to eat where we were going to eat, and He sat them right next to us, and He laid it on that man's heart to stand and pray the sweetest prayer.

It was the truth of Psalm 34:18 portrayed right before our eyes: *"The Lord is close to the brokenhearted and saves those who are crushed in spirit."*

### The Suicide Site

The events of the week seem like they were experienced while we were sleepwalking. From the trauma of the news that Shawn had committed suicide, the stress of the long trip, and not being particularly healthy to begin with, we were simply exhausted.

The activities of the next few days were very difficult, but they are days that we shall remember for a long time. For with the difficulties, came a number of God-hugs to remind us God was right beside us, taking each difficult step with us.

**God-hug 4: The Site.** After arriving on Sunday afternoon, we visited the site where Shawn had ended his life. On the

———

evening of May 23rd, 2012, he checked into a motel room, left a goodbye note to his wife and kids, then took his life in the vacant lot just south of the motel.

I was dreading how Ginny would react when we went to the site where her son committed suicide. I very much feared for her health at that point. I did not know if she would collapse in great heaving sobs as I had seen her do several times already, or just what she would do.

We walked slowly to the site, and once we arrived at the very place, you could see the imprints made by Shawn's heels as he dug himself into the loose dirt. He had scratched in the sand – "Free the spirit."

Ginny dropped to her knees, and placed her knees in the marks where Shawn had dug in his heels. She did not say anything for a minute or two, and then she said, "This is the last place where Shawn lived on earth. This is the place where he went to be with Jesus in Heaven. I know he is there right now."

There was a real peace that she seemed to have. She told me later that she deeply felt the presence of God as she knelt down there, and was so grateful that she knew that Shawn was with Jesus.

She remembered the day when, as a little boy, Shawn prayed a simple childlike prayer and asked Jesus to become his personal Savior. He did not know much about theology, but he knew that Jesus had died for his sin, and that he would be forgiven his sin by trusting Jesus as his Savior and Sin-bearer.

Being a Christian does not exempt us from the problems of life, nor does it guarantee us that we will not suffer the consequences of bad choices.

No parent could ever envision that the little boy sitting in her lap would one day find life so hopeless that he would end it himself. Our minds could never grasp such a thing.

How God turned our trip to that dreaded sight into a time of thanksgiving was a foretaste of what He would do for us the entire week. God knew that we could not handle this alone, so He met us in our great need with reassurances that He was a great God who gives great grace.

## *Can A Person Who Commits Suicide Go To Heaven?*

We have been referring to the fact that we believe with all our hearts that Shawn is in Heaven now. Are we just saying that to comfort ourselves, or do we have a Biblical basis for believing it?

There is a popular belief that those who commit suicide forfeit all chances of ever going to Heaven. The reasoning behind this belief is illustrated well by this statement from a well-meaning pastor that appeared on the Internet: "Suicide is sin, and one that cannot be repented of. When you commit suicide, you kill yourself, and you will be dead. Therefore you cannot repent, and you will go to hell for it."

At first glance, this thinking seems to sound reasonable, but reason is not the basis for solid belief – the Bible is! So, does the Bible speak to this subject? Is there Biblical teaching that is clear and precise? Yes, there is.

The Bible does teach that suicide is a sin, and it also teaches that one cannot enter Heaven with sin on his account. But this belief of having to "wipe our slate clean" just before we breathe our final breath is rooted in a misunderstanding of the vastness of God's forgiveness of sin found in His provision of Salvation.

---

The Bible teaches that the very moment we trust Jesus Christ to be our personal Savior, all of our sins are forgiven.

*"When you were dead in your sins...God made you alive with Christ. He forgave us all our sins"* (Colossians 2:13). *"He will have compassion upon us; he will subdue our iniquities; and thou wilt cast all their sins into the depths of the sea."* (Micah 7:19). *"Who gave himself for us, that he might redeem us from all iniquity."* (Titus 2:14)

Because God's provision of salvation forgives ALL our sins, past, present, and future, He can promise us, *"There is, therefore, now no condemnation to them who are in Christ Jesus."* Romans 8:1

There is "no condemnation" for the child of God because there is no sin on his account. ALL of his sins were paid in full at Calvary. That provision of absolute forgiveness became his at the moment of his salvation when, by faith, he received it as his own.

The promise of Heaven for the child of God is not dependent upon asking forgiveness for every unrepentant sin as he draws his final breath. There could be dozens of sins that we could forget to mention, or we might be killed instantly with no chance for a last minute confession.

Suicide is a sin, and those who commit suicide are indeed sinners – but the sin of suicide and all of our other sins were paid for in Christ's atonement. His death on the Cross paid the penalty for all sin for all time.

And those sinners who will trust God's provision of salvation can be as "confident" as the Scripture writer when he wrote: *"We are confident, I say, and willing rather to be absent from the body, and to be present with the Lord."* 2 Corinthians 5:8

———

Shawn was just a "sinner saved by grace" and at the moment of death, he was ushered by the angels into the presence of God. One day we will be reunited with him there.

Instead of staying at the house, we secured a motel room in the little town of Ozark. The confusion of all the people at the house and our special diet needs mandated that we locate ourselves where we could get some needed rest.

To be frank, I was really worried about Ginny's health. One look at her and you would have thought she had been hit by a Mac truck! Her eyes were swollen, her face was ashen, and she broke into sobs at the drop of a hat. She was grieving for herself, for her children who had lost their brother, and for Shawn's wife and four children.

As a Pastor of almost 30 years, I have been exposed to a lot of sorrow, but this was a whole new level of sorrow for me. I would literally have done anything to take some of the pain Ginny was carrying. All I could do was hold her, cry with her, listen, and oh yes, go to God on her behalf.

I remember thinking that week that it is funny how a person can think something is hard – then something harder comes along. I had thought that losing my job ten months earlier was a devastating event – then we lost a child.

I can tell you with no hesitation that the two losses are not on the same level. Pain is pain, I understand, but the pain of losing a child in the prime of his life at age 34 is unbearable. Especially since his death was by his own hand. The questions you are left with, the "if's," and the "I wish I would have known's" come like a flash flood.

*God-hug 5: The Coroner.* When active duty military personnel die on civilian property, as Shawn did, there is apparently a shared commitment of responsibility for funeral arrangements. We were told that Shawn would actually be having two funeral services, one military and the other civilian. We, of course, were invited to attend both. The two services were scheduled for Thursday morning.

On Tuesday we were informed that Shawn's body would be arriving at the local funeral home that day where they would be preparing his body for the funeral. That afternoon, Ginny asked me if we could drive by that funeral home. She said she just wanted to be near Shawn's body for a while.

We found the funeral home and as we drove by, Ginny asked if we couldn't just pull in the parking lot and sit for a while. I said sure we can.

After sitting in the car for 10 minutes, she said that she wondered if his body was there now. She said she would really like to go inside and be closer to where he was although she knew we had no chance of seeing his body.

Ginny's grandpa was a funeral director, and as a child she had been exposed to the inner workings of funerals and funeral directors. Her cousin even used to hide in the caskets and jump out and scare his cousins!

We walked to the door and knocked. A man in a suit came to the door, and I could see that he wore a badge with the name of the funeral home on it. We told him who we were and asked if we could come in a sit for just a few minutes.

Ginny explained to him who she was and said that if would be a real comfort to her just to sit in the same building where her son's body was at rest.

The nice gentleman came into the room where we were sitting, and asked if he could sit with us for a few minutes. He

———

then introduced himself as the County Coroner. He looked a little puzzled as he spoke to us, in that he said it was highly unusual that he was at this funeral home when we arrived. He said he was rarely ever there, but just had something he needed to pick up that morning.

He then told us that he had been on his way to Ozark a few days ago and received the call that a military person was down in the barren lot behind the motel. Then he told us that he was the one who had gone to the scene of Shawn's death and pronounced him dead.

For the next two hours this kind and gracious man shared with us, at Ginny's request, all the details surrounding the state of the body. He shared how military personnel had come to the scene to escort Shawn's body to the medical lab. He told us how they all had stood at attention and saluted Shawn, as his body was draped in an American flag and solemnly taken away. He told us it was a very respectful tribute to a fallen soldier.

There were tears of course as we listened, but there was a also a sense of deep gratitude that there had been such honor and tribute paid to Shawn's remains. What he shared with us was so comforting.

Ginny asked if Shawn would be presentable enough to have an open casket, and he assured her that Shawn was going to look very presentable. I might add here, that Shawn, dressed in his military uniform with all his medals, did indeed look really good.

We left the funeral home knowing that once again, our Heavenly Father had arranged circumstances to have us at just the right place at the just the right time to meet the man who was in charge of the suicide scene.

—

Dear friend, do you see what I mean when I tell you that, in the midst of this sorrow and loss, we were seeing the heart of God and the hand of God all around us?

It was as if on every corner God was telling us, "I am right here. I will not let you go through this alone. In your loss you will learn lessons about my love and care that will stay with you the rest of your life.

## The Funeral

Shawn's funeral(s) were held at the Army Chapel at Fort Rucker. The military funeral was first. It was such a fitting tribute to our son as his fellow soldiers stood, one by one, to give honor to their fallen comrade.

One part of the service took us by surprise. They called it the "Roll Call". In alphabetical order the names of Shawn's fellow soldiers were read. As their name was read, they answered, "Present."

When Shawn's name was read, there was silence of course. In fact the silence was absolutely deafening! Then his name was read once again, and the same silence followed. Then it was read a third time.

The point was made. He was absent. That was probably the most difficult part of the funeral for Ginny. What an encouragement though to realize that, although he was absent from us, he was *present with the Lord.*

He had been escorted to the arms of Jesus and was now more alive than he had ever been! He was at perfect peace in the presence of God - all sadness, pain, heartache, and confusion forever gone.

---

*God-hug 6: Afternoon Viewing.* Directly following the funeral at the Army chapel on base, we drove back to the little town of Ozark with some family to have lunch. Lane, Shawn's older brother, and Ginny's sister, Mary and her husband Gerry accompanied us.

Most of the restaurants were fast food with the exception of one buffet, which we were told had pretty good food.

We went through the line and were eating at our table when I noticed the funeral director and his staff entering the restaurant. I made my way to where they were in line to thank them for their part they conducted in the civilian funeral service.

For some reason the funeral director said to me, "You know, we will have Shawn's body at our funeral home all afternoon today. If Shawn's mother would care to see his body and say goodbye to him again, we would be happy to have you come. We will put in you a private room where you all can be alone."

So, when we finished our meal, we went to the funeral home where Shawn's casket was placed in a private room. It was such a special gift from God for Ginny to be able to be alone with him for a while away from all the noise and confusion.

What I witnessed that afternoon will stay with me forever.

Because Ginny grew up with close relatives who ran a funeral parlor, she had little hesitancy about being around a dead body. She approached the casket and touched Shawn's face, ran her fingers through his hair on the back of his neck. I had seen her do this countless times to her four "boys." It was a loving caress of a mother for her son.

Ginny is a very accomplished pianist. I have often told her

that she plays "with her heart on her fingertips." As she plays, you get a glimpse of the loving person she is inside, and her love for God.

That afternoon I saw the same flow of love from her heart to her fingertips to her son. It was sad, yet a beautiful thing to see. There was nothing morbid about it, just a time in which this loving mother with a broken heart was saying "Goodbye for now" to her son.

Ginny's sister and husband were in the room with us that afternoon, and we shared that private time together with them. Her sister, Mary, had lost her adult son just a year or so before. He had a terminal illness, and she had accompanied him to his doctor where he died in her arms at the doctor's office. Ginny did not have to explain to her how she felt – she already knew.

We are just so very grateful to God that He worked circumstances around in such a way that we could spend that time with Shawn's body. It brought a great closure to her. We looked at it as another God-hug, and could feel His presence with us while we were there.

Oh, some would say it was merely circumstantial that the funeral director happened to eat lunch at the same place and same time as we did that day. Some would say too that his kind offer to let us view the body privately was not out of the ordinary, but in thirty years of officiating funerals, I had never heard of that happening.

Isn't it is just as plausible to believe there is a loving Heavenly Father Who once again went out of His way to minister to our breaking hearts. Would it be too hard to imagine that God can control the circumstances in order to let us know in a very special way that He loved us and was near us?

## *The Burial Service*

Shawn's body was to be laid to rest at the military cemetery in Pensacola, Florida on Friday. The funeral director took us aside and told us that the plan was for everyone to drive in a procession to the burial. He said there would be a large "wounded warriors" motorcycle group accompanying us. He said that we would be leaving around 7AM, and for us to expect about a four-hour drive.

Ginny had not been feeling well before we left Iowa and especially on the way down to Alabama. We had made numerous stops along the way because of it. When she was told that there was going to be a four-hour procession to the burial site, she looked somewhat panicked.

She immediately thought of how embarrassing it was going to be if she caused the entire procession to stop numerous times along the route. This would be most embarrassing and draw attention to her in a way that she did not want.

A military officer approached Ginny immediately after the funeral director gave us the news about the processional to the burial. I am not sure if he saw Ginny's reaction to this news or if he just thought she looked ill, but he made this offer to us.

He said, "Mrs. Garnett, there is an alternative to you having to make the long trip to Pensacola, "If you would prefer, we can have one of our officers conduct a private service in your home in Iowa just for you and your family. The service will be honoring to your son, and we will present you with the very same American flag that you would be receiving tomorrow.
What a Godsend! In light of Ginny's physical and emotional condition, this option was very appealing to her. We could return home, get some rest, and later have a final tribute for Shawn in the privacy of our own home.

---

She would not have to make this long, four-hour trip to Pensacola and four-hour trip back. She would not have to take the risk of being embarrassed by stopping the processional several times along the way.

She knew the Pensacola service would be lovely, but at that time she was totally exhausted, and readily chose the option of having a private service in our home in Iowa.

We said our goodbyes to family and friends, and left for Iowa on Friday morning. We had not gotten to bed until around 2 a.m. the previous night, and my diabetes was putting me in somewhat of a stupor. I simply could not stay awake to drive.

This put all the pressure on Ginny to drive the long way home. We are so grateful for God's provision of safety over us on the long trip home.

We did not count them, but I would guess the stops we made coming home must have numbered in the 30's! We arrived home around 2 PM on Saturday afternoon, and went straight to bed.

## *Military Ceremony At Home*

After a few days, an Army officer, Major Kelly Scott, contacted us. In our first meeting with him at our house, he shared how he had given his life to Christ a few years ago, and how God had turned his life around. Ginny and I both had a connection with him immediately.

Major Scott had served in Iraq back in 2003-04 as a commander/medical logistician and suffered from minor symptoms PTSD upon returning home, so when he learned that PTSD was the contributing factor to Shawn's suicide, he understood the difficulty that Shawn had gone through.

A week later, on a Sunday afternoon, Major Kelly Scott arrived at our home dressed in his full "color blues." He carried with him a very beautifully crafted wooden triangular box with the American flag folded neatly inside. On the inside lid of the box was a display of all of Shawn's military medals, awards, and insignias. They appeared in exactly the same placement as they appeared when Shawn wore them on his chest.

Major Scott noticed that Shawn's 101st Airborne insignia was missing. He told us he would be honored to give us his own Airborne insignia so the display would be complete. We were touched. He removed his insignia from his own chest full of medals and added it to the rack of medals in the display case.

He commented several times at the four "Air Medals" that Shawn had earned, one of which had a "V" device for Valor. He said Shawn was more highly decorated than any 34-year-old soldier he had ever seen.

We had never heard anything about any of this from Shawn. While he was deployed four times, he was always "doing really good" when he wrote or talked to his mom. We know now that he just did not want to worry her.

A solemn and beautiful ceremony was conducted. "Taps" were played as Major Scott stood at attention and saluted. Then with tears running down his face, he knelt and presented Ginny with the flag box and medals. It was a very touching experience giving a wonderful tribute to Shawn and his selfless service to his country.

Our son, Mickey, and our daughter, Summer, were able to join us for this private service to honor their brother.

### God Continues To Show Up In Everyday Life
Someone once said, "No sorrow ever leaves you where it finds you; it either drives you from God or drives you to Him." The

next days and weeks were extremely hard for Ginny, but at their core was a steadfast assurance that God was right there with us, sustaining us, and giving us His peace.

*God-hug 7: Car Expenses.* One such instance had to do with car repairs on Ginny's 2006 Impala. We had taken it to the dealer where we purchased it, Karl's Chevrolet, because we have always appreciated the quality of their service.

The problems were analyzed and one of their servicemen called with the news. "You need about $1800 worth of repairs," he said.

Not good! We had just had all the expenses to Alabama, and the timing on this news could not have been worse! I told him to hold off doing anything on the car, and I would get back to him in a couple of hours. We discussed whether it would be worth putting $1800 into a 2006 car that was only worth $6000.

We had not made a decision yet when the phone rang again – it was the man from Karl's.

"I have an offer for you," he said. "If you will pay $192 to align your car, we will cover the rest of the expense!"

I could not believe what I was hearing! "Why on earth would you do that," I asked him. Why would you absorb over $1600 worth of expenses for us?"

"Do you know us?" I asked.

"No, I don't think so." he answered.

"Did you hear anything about us recently?" I continued.
"Like what?" he said.

"We just lost our 34 year-old Army son – he had PTSD and

—

committed suicide. We just got back from his funeral in Alabama."

It was quiet. Then he said, "No, I did not know that. I am so sorry for your loss. We are offering to do this for you just because we are Karl's, and we can."

Karl's is the biggest Chevy dealership West of the Mississippi! They are not a small, family dealership where they know all their customers. I was totally amazed at the offer.

My voice cracked with emotion, and I said to the serviceman, "I am a Christian. These past few days have been so difficult for us. I am looking at your offer as just another way that God is telling us that He is here with us – right by our side."

The man was silent, as he spoke, his voice cracked, "I am a believer too. I really never expected God to use me to do something like this, but I have to agree with you – it seems like He is behind this."

And with that, I gave him the "go ahead" to fix our car. We picked it up a day later, paid the $192 bill and drove it home with over $1800 worth of repairs on it!

God does not always work that way, but sometimes He does. I am just trying to show you that at times, God does things for us because we desperately need to know in a special way that He is there.

Six months later Ginny's heater went out on the same car. It cost $645 to fix it, and we paid the entire bill. We did not expect God to pay it for us. We were just grateful He had done that once – when we were really needing to know He was right at our side.

—

## Military Help

*God-hug 8: Travel Costs.* The costs incurred in traveling to Alabama, food, and staying in a motel for a week were substantial. We always knew that, if necessary, we could take money out of our savings, but with our reduced income were very cautious about doing so.

We had put most of the travel expenses on our credit card, but before the bill arrived, the Army notified us that they were going to cover all the travel expenses! We could hardly believe it.

Major Kelly explained that that is what the Army does when one of their active soldiers dies. They cover all the costs of travel, lodging, and meals. In fact, they did so, for not only Ginny and me, but also for Shawn's brothers and sisters.

We gathered all our receipts together, submitted them, and were promptly reimbursed. What an unexpected blessing!

*God-hug 9: Our Wills.* The Army also told us that they would offer us the services of one of their local JAG's (Judge Advocate General). This is an officer who is also an attorney, who would help us with re-writing our wills or any other legal work we needed done. We availed ourselves of this kind offer.

The Army also offered to cover the cost of any counseling we needed. This was something that a number of people told us we should do, and we were open to this possibility.

But after both of us prayed about God's leading in the matter, God once again impressed on us a passage in 1 Samuel 30.

This time God emphasized the extreme duress David was under, *"David and the people lifted up their voice and wept, until they had no more power to weep"* (v.4), and God's provision for David, *"David encouraged himself in the Lord His God"* (v.6b)

We feel that professional counseling is certainly appropriate in many situations, but at that time, we felt God wanted us to have Him serve as our Counselor. Again, we would have been happy to pursue counseling, but just did not feel that it was the path God wanted us to travel at that time. Maybe there will be a time in the future where that is needed. If so, we will not hesitate to pursue it.

### *Unlikely Prayer Partners*

I was concerned about Ginny's health for the next few weeks. She had lost a considerable amount of weight because she felt nauseated most of the time. It was necessary for me to stay close to her, because when I left her side she would have a panic attack.

If you have ever gone through a tragedy of this magnitude, you will know that symptoms like this do not mean you do not have faith in God. They mean you are human. Ginny was so run down physically and emotionally that she could not sleep at night or during the day, and she could not eat.

Her emotions were raw, and when we went out in public, it was not unusual for her to burst into tears. She told me that her chest physically hurt from the pain she felt in her heart.

**God-hug 10: Olive Garden.** We were sitting at Olive Garden one noon and were just about to order. As the young waiter approached, Ginny started to weep. The poor young man was a bit bewildered. I felt sorry for him.

As Ginny cried, I explained to him that our military son had just committed suicide, and we were just back from his funeral.

---

The young man got down on one knee beside our booth and said, "I go to the Bible College here in town and am planning on being a pastor some day. I believe God brought you in here today so I could begin to pray for you."

With that, he bowed his head and prayed softly for us that God would comfort us in our grief and somehow mend our broken hearts.

*God-hug 11: Girl at the Lake.* Another instance occurred like this while I was across the street fishing in our little lake in the community park. A young lady passed by me as I fished from the bridge. I noticed she was carrying her Bible.

She asked me if I were catching anything, and I told her no, but it didn't matter. I was actually just enjoying the tranquility of the lake. She agreed that it was very peaceful.

Because I noticed her Bible, I told her our Army son had just committed suicide, and that we were just back from his funeral. She told me how sorry she was and that she would pray for us. Then she went on her way.

About 20 minutes later she came back across the bridge and said to me, "I was reading this passage of Scripture this morning and I feel like God gave it to me to share with you." She read the passage to me and promised that she would be praying for us in the days ahead.

I do not remember what the passage was, but I know it had something to do about God taking care of us in time of trouble because He loved us so much.

I have been on that bridge dozens of times since, but have never seen the young lady again.

Could it be that God sent her there that morning to remind us that He was right beside us and was going to help us get through this? I do not know, but I do know how much of a blessing it was to have things like this happen.

God-Hugs - constant reminders to us that God's presence, God's peace, and God's Promises were close by.

# Part Four

## The Bottom Really Wasn't The Bottom

## *This Cannot Be Happening!*

Shawn's suicide took place on May 24, 2012. By the first of July, Ginny was doing better physically. She had started eating more normally and was sleeping better than she had for weeks. I guess you could say we were starting to experience a new "normal."

There seemed to be something that the Army required us to do every three or four days, so there were constant meetings with Major Scott involving a lot of signing and looking at paperwork.

Of course there were still times of deep sadness and sorrow. There were still times of weeping. There were times when neither of us could go to bed and stay there at night.

Nonetheless, I could see that there was some improvement in Ginny's health and demeanor.

Around 8:30PM, on Wednesday, July 4th, the phone rang. The caller ID said it was our daughter Melissa. Melissa lived in Virginia Beach, VA, with her pastor husband, Steve, and their three kids.

Had Shawn not taken his life, we were supposed to drive to Melissa's in June and spend a week with her. We were just so exhausted after the funeral and the trip home, we canceled the trip to Melissa's.

Ginny and Melissa were very close. Although she left home and Iowa at age 18 to travel to Florida to work as a nanny, she kept in touch with us a lot. After a couple of years she began teaching at a Christian school, and eventually married the pastor of the church that owned and ran the school.

As often happens, Pastors feel God calling them to a new field of service, so after about five years or so, Melissa and her

---

husband Steve moved to Virginia Beach, Va. There, Steve served as a church planter, and they started their family.

Each time another child would be born, Ginny and I would travel to Virginia Beach and do what we could to help out. That normally consisted of Ginny helping Melissa recoup from the C-Section and assume the household responsibilities for a week to ten days. I, on the other hand, served as the "new baby holder."

Once the baby had been fed, changed, and ready for a nap, it was "Grandpa time." I very much enjoyed just holding the little one in my arms. I knew he could just as well sleep by himself, so my contribution was more for my enjoyment than his needs.

I was honored beyond words when Steve and Melissa announced that they were going to name their third, and last child, after me. "Jameson" bears my name and will be a forever reminder to the relationship God gave me with Melissa.

Melissa was about sixteen years old, and her sister Summer, fourteen, when I married their mom. I proceeded very cautiously in my new role as their stepdad, feeling that I needed to earn their love and devotion, not demand it. I made many mistakes along the way, but they forgave every one of them. Our blended family (including my two kids and Ginny's other four kids) grew to love and respect each other.

Over the course of time, I came to sincerely think of Melissa and Summer as my own daughters.

Melissa was married with kids when I asked her to consider writing the Foreword to a new book. It would be called "How

To Blend Your Blended Family". It was easy to tell people how to do it since I had made so many mistakes myself in actually doing it. All I needed to do was tell them to do it the opposite way I had done it!

In asking Melissa to write the Foreword, I wanted the readers to see a blended family and its challenges through the eyes of one of the kids. I was very shocked to see the natural writing ability that Melissa showed. I was even more shocked to see how she honored me by the kind words she chose. Here's an excerpt from her Foreword:

*"As you'll see in the book, children and parents go through many unique changes as multiple families attempt to blend into one. While going through these changes in my life, I was fortunate to have a step-dad that understood what I was going through. He treated my mom in a way that she had never been treated before, with love and respect. He also reached out to me with love and patience. My step-dad did such a tremendous job. Jim Garnett is not only my "step-dad," he is the only father I have ever had. Just like it says in this book, we were able to move beyond that "step" relationship. He is my father in every aspect of the word, and I love him dearly."*

Wow! Her words caught me totally off guard, and I remember weeping as I read it the first time.

Ginny and Melissa would talk two or three times a week. It was customary when Ginny's cell phone would ring that we would look at each other and say "Melissa."

Melissa was so willing to share with us about the kids, and the normal routine of life. We loved it. She was always sending us pictures of the kids, and kept Grandma Ginny and Grandpa Jim as very real entities before her children. She knew how much we loved them and wanted to be involved in their lives as they grew.

—

## "She Needs To Hear Your Voice"

By the look on Ginny's face, I could tell that something was very wrong. The call was from Melissa's husband, Steve, who was calling on Melissa's cell phone. Here is the story of what happened in Ginny's own words.

*"Steve asked me if Jim was with me, and when I said, "Yes," he asked me to put the call on speaker phone."*

*"Steve started by saying, "I am at the hospital in Norfolk with Melissa. I cannot answer your questions right now. She has attempted to take her life. Right now she is struggling to stay alive. The doctor needs her to wake up, but we cannot get her to do so. I thought maybe hearing your voice, Miss Ginny, would help. Will you talk to her while I hold the phone to her ear?"*

*"I was in total shock. I asked God to give me strength and help me talk."*

*"I quietly spoke Melissa's name into the phone. I could hear Steve say, "She woke up!"*

*"I went on to tell her how much I loved her and to just hang on because we would try to see her as soon as possible."*

*"Steve told me that Melissa desperately tried to grab the phone, but because she had a breathing tube down her throat, she could not talk. I just kept telling her how much I loved her, and that we would be praying for her."*

*"Steve took the phone and told me that they were going to transfer Melissa by helicopter to a hospital in Richmond VA, that specialized in liver transplants. That was what needed to be done to save her life. He asked me to stand-by just in case they had to call me again to talk to Melissa to get her to wake up. "Then Steve had to go. That was all the details we had for the time being."*

—

When Ginny hung up the phone, we just looked at each other with unbelief! Had we really received a phone call telling us that another of our children had tried to kill themselves? It just could not be possible – could it?

It was simply beyond belief that another one of our kids had attempted suicide. Shawn was messed up from PTSD, but not Melissa. She was a beautiful, outgoing mother of three, who seemed to love life, her family, and God. What could possibly have been so wrong that she thought it was better to end her life than go on?

In the midst of all this confusion and chaos, we knew that God was still right by our side. We could feel His presence and would occasionally remind each other of the precious promises He had given us.

## *Hopeful, Then No Hope*

Neither of us slept much that night. We looked at flights on the Internet to see if we could leave right away, but also wanted to be reachable in case Steve needed to get hold of Ginny again soon.

Reports of improvement came to us the next day from the doctors at the Richmond hospital. They felt that Melissa had reached them in time, and that with a liver transplant would eventually recover.

Steve called again Thursday morning and asked Ginny to once again speak to Melissa on the phone and try to wake her up. Again, here are Ginny's own words of what happened:

*"I said, Melissa, this is Mom," and I heard everyone in the room become excited because she did wake up again. I poured out my love to her again, telling her that we would be there soon."*

*"Steve got on the phone again and asked me to direct Melissa to*

---

squeeze his hand. I could tell by the excitement in the room that she had done what I asked. Everyone was so hopeful that Melissa would have the liver transplant that day – and they did secure a liver for her which, we thought, was quite a miracle in itself."

"As I said goodbye to Melissa, I promised her that we would see her soon. Steve's last words to me were that things seemed to be going well, and he was very hopeful that the liver transplant would save her life."

"I decided it was now time to call my children to tell them the awful news about their sister. With each call came the same questions – questions for which I had no answers."

"The events of this time are a blur of confusion and chaos. On Saturday morning we received another call. As they were preparing Melissa for liver surgery, the doctor walked into her room and shared that Melissa had suffered a heart attack earlier. This showed up when they were checking everything to make sure her body was ready for the transplant."

"The doctor told them that they could not perform a liver transplant on someone who had suffered a heart attack and was not well enough to receive it. What had seemed like a hopeful situation had quickly turned to a situation with no hope."

"Steve told me that we should come right away so we could see Melissa alive."

Immediately we tried to get a plane out of Des Moines, but there were absolutely no flights going to Richmond until early Sunday morning. So we booked tickets, packed our bags, and paced back and forth. We prayed and asked God to keep Melissa alive until we got there.

We turned in early Saturday night, but after an hour got back up, showered, and stayed up the rest of the night. We simply

—

could not sleep.

## The Trip To Say "Goodbye"

About 4AM we headed to the airport. We took Ginny's car, so she drove. About a mile from the airport I noticed that our car seemed to be heading toward the center median. I said, "Ginny, what are you doing!"

She responded, "I was asleep. Sorry." Thank God for His guardian angels! I think ours decided to get out and walk after our trip to the airport that morning.

We could not correspond with Steve while we were on the plane, but when we landed in Chicago, just before noon, Ginny called Steve and found out that Melissa was still alive.

The flight arrived in Richmond around 2PM, and rather than take time to rent a car, we took the first taxi we could find. I encouraged the driver to drive as fast as he could because our daughter was in the hospital.

As the taxi pulled up in front of the hospital, I told Ginny to go ahead, and I would pay for the taxi and get our bags. She ran to the hospital and waited at the steps for me. We ran into the hospital and stopped at the front desk to get Melissa's room number. We headed to the elevator, which took forever to go up three floors, and when the door opened, we shot out.

We asked a nurse where we should go and headed down a hallway. We passed a room on the left and I said, "Wait Ginny! I think that is Steve's sister sitting in that room."

Once again, Ginny describes the events in her own words:
*"I stopped quickly to look and did recognize Steve's sister. I took one look at her face and said, "She's gone, isn't she? "   She nodded slowly and said, "About 15 minutes after you took off from Chicago, her blood pressure started to drop.  Steve was able to be with her as*

---

*she took her last breaths, but she died about 2 hours ago. "*

*"I remember just bursting uncontrollably into sobs as I commented, 'I just can't go through this again.' I buried my face in my hands and sobbed for a long time. I couldn't stop crying. I was completely in shock and so very sad and just didn't know what to do. Finally I started to settle down after about 20 minutes and asked if I could please see my daughter."*

## *Too Late*

There is surely some type of "button" that God equips us with that shuts us down when life is offering us more than we can possibly handle. The next minutes were like a movie running in slow motion.

Our beautiful daughter that we had just seen six weeks before was now lying in a hospital bed all by herself. She had taken her life, leaving behind a husband and three children. Surely this was a cruel dream. We would wake soon to find that none of this had actually happened.

But it was not a dream. It was real. The bottom dropped out of life when Shawn committed suicide. Now we were finding that the bottom wasn't really the bottom at all. Ginny writes:

*"The doctor walked us down the hall. My mind was racing, trying to imagine what I was going to have to see. But I needed to see Melissa one more time – I had held her the minute I had given birth to her, and I needed to be able to say goodbye. They had disconnected all the hoses and tubes. The doctor entered the room with us, but we asked her to leave so we could be alone with Melissa."*

*"I went to her side and just stared at her. I then cradled her in my arms and ran my fingertips over her face, looking for any sign of life. Her temples were still warm, which comforted me. I played with her hair, as I had done all of her life. I touched her arms, her hands and just wanted to hang on to her forever. Her eyes were closed, and I*

---

*knew I would never again see her look at me. It broke my heart into a thousand little pieces. My chest actually ached with pain it hurt so much. I gently lifted her eyelids to take one final look at her beautiful face with her eyes open. There was simply no life in them. I just stood there for quite awhile, not wanting to admit that she was really dead."*

I stood at the foot of her bed just looking at Melissa. I was now at a total loss to know what to do or what to say. The only words I could get to come out of my mouth was, "Melissa, Melissa, Melissa, what have you done?"

We held each other tight and wept. We talked to Melissa and told her there was absolutely nothing she could ever do that would keep us from loving her. We told the Lord that we were thankful she was now in His presence, and that He would look after her until we would see her again. We told God that we knew she and Shawn were together again, and they both were with their Grandpa Ray and also with Jesus.

I really do not remember much more that happened in those minutes and hours. The events of that day coupled with the events of the last month put us in a state of "absolute overload."

### *Déjà Vu*

Those friends, who had stayed with Melissa until we arrived, left to drive back to Virginia Beach within the hour. We rented a room at a Richmond hotel. Once settled in the room, Ginny began the difficult task of calling her children to tell them the sad news of their sister's death.

Time seemed to go in slow motion. Only a month before I had witnessed this same gut-wrenching scene. Ginny would try to get herself collected enough so she could be strong for her children, but with the first words of each new call, she would

---

collapse into great heaving sobs. To watch my beautiful wife go through this was frankly, more than I thought she could take. I saw once again a level of pain that I had never seen before, and one I certainly hope I never witness again.

I had thought that the first time this happened, it was enough pain to last a lifetime, but we were now going through it all again.

Three of the kids were attending a function in the Quad Cities, so were together when the news of Melissa's death came. Melissa's older brother was just a mile away from the others, so the three went to his house. There they cried, and held onto each other, and prayed for Melissa's husband and children, for us, and for themselves.

We had received word that Melissa's funeral would be on Saturday, but decided to stay in our quiet location in Richmond until Thursday, then drive to Virginia Beach where the funeral would be held.

A few mornings after Melissa's death, Ginny and I were eating breakfast in the kitchen area of the Richmond motel. CNN was running a story about a teenager who had been swept away to his death by a big ocean wave. They were interviewing his mother.

I remember looking across the table at Ginny and saying, "It must be an awful thing to lose one of your kids." Then, of course, it hit me like a ton of bricks - we had lost a child – 2 of them! We could identify the sorrow and pain we saw on this mother's face. We knew what she was going through. No explanation was necessary.

On Thursday we drove to Virginia Beach, and went to Melissa's house to spend time with Melissa's husband, Steve,

—

their three children, and our kids who were arriving for the funeral.

Melissa's funeral was on Saturday. After the funeral we ate lunch with several of our kids, drove back to Richmond, and the next day we flew out of Richmond for home.

———

# Part Five

*Photo Memories of Shawn and Melissa*

Lane, Melissa, Kory, Summer, Shawn, and Mickey

Ginny and her "boys" on the banks of the Mississippi in June, 2010

Ginny and Shawn next to his helicopter – June 2007

Shawn and Ginny in
December 2003

Shawn hanging out with brothers Kory,
Lane, and Mickey

Ginny and Shawn by the military monument in LeClaire, Iowa

Display at Shawn's funeral – his flying helmet, rifle, boots, and dog tags.

The remaining five children and Ginny at Shawn's casket.

Ginny and the five remaining children at Shawn's funeral.

Mickey consoles his sisters, Summer and Melissa.

Major Kelly Scott presents Ginny with a flag during a private ceremony in our home.

Melissa and her brothers Shawn, Mickey, Lane, and Kory

Melissa had just told Ginny she was pregnant with her first child,

Youngest to the oldest: Summer, Melissa, Shawn, Kory, Mickey. (Lane, the oldest, is absent)

Melissa's 30<sup>th</sup> birthday and my 60<sup>th</sup>.

Mickey and Melissa

Another birthday picture.

Melissa

Melissa at Panera Bread.

Melissa and me during high school years.

Melissa was never too old to sit on
Mommy's lap!

Ginny, Melissa, and me.

—

# Part Six

*Life After Deaths –*
*The New Normal*

## *How Did You Make It Through?*

Today is July 13, 2013. It has been nearly two years since I lost my job, and one year since our two kids committed suicide. It has been a time wherein we have suffered greater losses than we ever knew before.

We really believe that these losses were experienced under the watchful eye of our Father. That does not make the losses easy, but it does give some sense of purpose to them. We do not know the purposes, but we do not have to know. We know our Father, and He knows the purposes.

I read years ago, "When you cannot trace the hand of God, you can trust the heart of God." He is, indeed, too loving to be unkind, and too wise to make mistakes.

The comment we have heard more than any other over the last year is, "I really don't know how you guys are getting through this."

I have at times made that comment to other people over the years, when in the midst of their difficulties, I tried to put myself in their place and could not relate to their level of suffering or how they were surviving.

So, God began to speak to me and direct me along the path of letting people know how we survived such loss. What did we do, or what was done for us that helped us make it through? Maybe if I can share some answers along those lines, it will help someone else know how to make it through. It might also help others know what to do to make a difference in the lives of those who are suffering.

So, here is a simple explanation of some of the things we did, some of the things God did, and some of the things others did to help us survive in the midst of the deep waters.

———

# 1. The Provision of Grace

We have begun to realize a very precious truth about God's grace – it is not given to us before we need it. It is not supplied in advance and stored up to be used later. It is given to us at the time we need it.

His grace comes with our need. We are not given grace to understand how someone else makes it through, only how we will make it through.

It is like the provision of food that God miraculously provided the widow who took care of his prophet Elijah. You recall there was great famine, and yet when Elijah first met the widow, he asked her to make him a little cake from the meal that she had left in her barrel. She was about to make one last cake for her and her son with that meal, but instead she did as Elijah asked and prepared a cake for him first.

After she had done so, Elijah said to her, "this is what the LORD, the God of Israel, says: The jar of flour will not be used up and the jug of oil will not run dry until the day the LORD sends rain on the land. She went away and did as Elijah had told her. So there was food every day for Elijah and for the woman and her family. For the jar of flour was not used up and the jug of oil did not run dry, in keeping with the word of the LORD spoken by Elijah." (1 Kings 17:14-16 NIV)

So, what do you envision as you read what occurred during the days Elijah stayed with this widow? Do you envision a filled up jar of flour and a big jug of oil filled to the brim? If so, you have not seen it correctly.

This is what occurred. Every time the widow would bake bread she would go to the jar of flour that was just about out and the jug of oil that was just about empty. There was just enough – but there was always enough.

---

Her faith had to be exercised each meal to believe when she used what she needed, God would replenish what was taken with more. The right amount was always there, but there was none extra to store up for later. She was given the provision of flour and oil when she needed it – not before and not a second too late.

That also is how God supplied "manna" to the children of Israel for 40 years as they wandered in the wilderness. Manna means, "What is it?" That is what the children of Israel said the first time they saw it. When they awoke it was laying on the ground, and they looked at it and said, "Manna (what is it)?"

God told them they would have to gather this honey-tasting wafer every day for that day's need. On Friday they could gather enough for the Saturday (the Sabbath) too, but if they tried to gather more than one day's provision, it would be rotten before they could use the rest.

God's provision to us comes like that, dear friend – one day at a time, one step at a time. His grace is never given to us beyond more than what we need right then. It is never given in such a way that we can store it up and use it later.

There is just enough for now! But there is always enough for now!

God has taught us that these past two years. That is usually how He supplies our needs – enough grace for right now.

I do not have all the answers as to why God works in the ways He does, but I can tell you this – that method requires us to keep trusting God each day. We can never quit exercising faith because His provision is not for tomorrow, just today.

We cannot trust the provision – we must trust the Provider.

———

We have to believe that He is able and willing to supply all we will need for this step and the next.

Isn't that what living by faith is all about? Sure it is. But we often have to be brought to that place in our life where we realize how weak we are and how unable we are – before we will quit trusting in ourselves and start trusting in God.

That does seem to be the teaching of 2 Corinthians 12:9, "My grace is sufficient for you, for my power is made perfect in weakness." Grace is supplied at the time of our "weakness", not days or months before. It is at the time when circumstances beat us down, and we cannot take another step. Then God's grace is supplied to carry us. At the moment of our greatest need, we find God sufficient.

We wonder how we could ever make it if what happened to "them" would happen to us, but we will never know until it actually happens to us and God's grace is supplied. Grace is given and experienced when needed, not before.

One day I saw a little article I had pasted in the cover page of my Bible nearly 25 years before. It was the testimony of the great 19th century English preacher, Charles Haddon Spurgeon, as he came to realize the sufficiency of God's grace.

"The other evening as I was riding home after a heavy day's work, I felt very wearied, and sore depressed, when swiftly and suddenly as a lightning flash, that text came to me, 'My grace is sufficient for thee."

*"I reached home and looked it up in the original (Greek language), and at last it came to me in this way "MY grace is sufficient for thee;" and I said, "I should think it is Lord." and burst out laughing. I never fully understood what the holy laughter of Abraham was until then. It seemed to make unbelief so absurd!"*

———

*"It was as though some little fish, being very thirsty, was troubled about drinking the river dry, and Father Thames said, "Drink away, little fish, my stream is sufficient for thee." or, it seemed after the seven years of plenty, a mouse feared it might die of famine; and Joseph might say, "Cheer up, little mouse, my granaries are sufficient for thee." Again, I imagined a man way up yonder in a lofty mountain saying to himself, "I breathe so many cubic feet of air every year, I fear I shall exhaust the oxygen in the atmosphere." but the earth says, "Breathe away, O man, and fill the lungs ever, my atmosphere is sufficient for thee." Oh, brethren, be great believers! Little faith will bring your souls to heaven, but great faith will bring heaven to your souls."*

How did we make it through? It was by the Provision of God's Grace given to us at just the right time and in just the right amount.

## 2. The Praise We Offered God

Another way that Ginny and I were able to get through each day involved a rather unusual discovery that had to do with praise. We found that there is a correlation between God's presence and our praise.

We came across this truth through some special songs that God used to minister to us. Not only did they bring a sweet peace to our hearts, they also taught us about a Biblical teaching concerning God's presence.

One day we heard a song that Ginny used to play in church years before. It has an unusual phrase in the chorus that especially caught my attention now, "Praise the Lord, for our God inhabits praise."

The songwriter borrowed this thought from Psalm 22:3, "But Thou art holy, O Thou that inhabits the praises of Israel." (KJV)

———

Another version translates this statement, "But you are holy, enthroned in the praises of Israel."

I became fascinated with what this verse was saying, and read a number of commentaries to glean the thoughts of learned men. One dear pastor had preached an entire message on the phrase. In doing so he revealed how difficult it is to translate the Hebrew words accurately, and difficult to understand their exact meaning.

I paraphrase His final conclusion: "I do not understand yet what it means when the verse tells us that God inhabits the praise of Israel – that He is enthroned in Israel's praise. If I were to explain the meaning in simple words, it is this: "When you praise God, He shows up!"

That explanation made sense to me, and we began to practice what it was teaching. We found out experientially, that in the darkest of times, when it feels like your heart hurts so much it is going to break, if you will simply and sincerely begin to give God praise, He "shows up!"

And when He shows up, the situation begins to take on a new meaning. We may not understand the why's or the wherefore's, but we have a calm assurance that He is in control.

Praise allows us to focus on what He has done, and what He can do. It lifts our eyes and our hearts above the circumstances - up to the place where God is seated on His Heavenly Throne. Up to the place where there is peace and solace.

### 3. The Prospect of Heaven

Another way that helped us cope with the losses of our two kids is the truth of Matthew 6:21. There Jesus said, *"For where your treasure is, there will your heart be also."* In other words, our **interest** will follow our **investment**.

———

Ginny and I now had an additional investment in Heaven – two of our children – and that seemed to stimulate our interest in Heaven even more.

They had both trusted Jesus as their Savior and Sin-Bearer when they were young. At that moment, according to Colossians 2:13 "*all*" of their sins were forgiven. As we said before, this means, not just their past sins, but their sins in the present and sins in the future. *All* their sins, even the sin of suicide.

They were gone from us, but we knew where they were. They were now in the presence of the Lord Jesus in Heaven.

Songs about Heaven became more real to us. Bible passages about Heaven took on a new meaning. We also found ourselves reading books about Heaven

Three of those books that we found particularly intriguing were "*Heaven Is For Real: A Little Boy's Astounding Story of His Trip To Heaven and Back*" by Todd Burpo, "*Have Heart*" written by Steve and Sarah Berger, a couple who suffered the tragic loss of their 19-year-old son, Josiah, and "*Heaven*" by Randy Alcorn, the most thorough discussion of heaven ever written.

We realized that as one gets older, heaven becomes populated with immediate family members, relatives, and close friends. But now we had two children there.

We often would ask each other, "I wonder what Shawn and Melissa are doing in Heaven right now?"

We would think out loud as to whom they had met and what they were doing. We figured they had met the Lord Jesus right at first but wondered if they were spending time with their Grandpa Ray, Ginny's dad. We wondered if they had conversed with Moses or Abraham or Paul. We figured by now that they had met their older brother or sister who was miscarried before they were born.

Occasionally we would ask Jesus to look them up and put His arms around them and tell them we are looking forward to seeing them again soon. We knew we could not communicate with them, but we could communicate with Someone who saw them every day – Jesus.

It was about a year after Melissa's death that Ginny made a comment that surprised me. She said, "I emailed Melissa again the other day." When I asked her about it she told me that occasionally she writes Melissa an email and expresses her thoughts to her.

We thought it might be of help to someone reading this material if you could see what she wrote, so with Ginny's permission I will share them with you.

*****************************************

7/5/2012

My Sweet Melissa,
You have been in my prayers all night. I have prayed that God will fold you in His arms and heal you so that you will be ok. You were such a gift to me almost 33 years ago. I pray that I will see you open your eyes and talk. I don't have the right words right now, but just know that I love you and need you to be OK.

Hang on, Sweetheart!! I hope to see you soon.

Love, Mom

\*\*\*\*\*\*\*\*\*\*\*\*\*\*\*\*\*\*\*\*\*\*\*\*\*\*\*\*\*\*\*\*\*\*\*\*\*\*\*\*

8/04/2012

Dear Sweet Melissa,
I miss you so much. It's been a whole month, and I'm just wanting to talk to you and hug you and tell you I love you. You're my little girl. You are the joy of my life. I know you must be experiencing so many unimaginable things in heaven. I long to be there some day and see Jesus face to face---and see your smiling face. When I think of the comfort and peace you have now, it makes me feel better because I know that you are perfect now. You are happy and you get to be with all of our loved ones and friends that are in heaven, too. So many things happen here on earth, and I want to pick up the phone and share them with you. We did that a lot, didn't we??!!

Every time my phone rings now, I just always look to see if it's you. I am sad because I know it isn't. But God is helping me-- His word is full of letters from Him to help us thru our grief and sadness. You are with Shawn, too. I miss him so much, too, even though we didn't talk as often as you and I did. I know both of you are safe in the arms of Jesus. I just needed to write and tell you I love you and always will. Bye for now, my lovely daughter!!

Lots of love from Mom

\*\*\*\*\*\*\*\*\*\*\*\*\*\*\*\*\*\*\*\*\*\*\*\*\*\*\*\*\*\*\*\*\*\*\*\*\*\*\*\*

10/30/2012

Dear Sweet Melissa,

Today is your baby girl's 6th birthday, and it is breaking my heart, so thought I would just write to you to see if that helps. I want to hold her and reassure her that everything will be all right. I just miss you so much myself that I can't imagine what your kids must feel. I still have so many questions, and always will. It does no good to write those down--I just want this awful ache inside of me to disappear. I wish I could hold you in my arms again and reassure you too, that everything will be ok. The thing is, I know you ARE perfect now--you are home with Jesus. So I have to concentrate on that and look forward even more to the day when I will join you and Shawn, my 2 precious kids, and see Jesus for myself. What a day that will be. That really does encourage me.

So I will probably talk to Steve and see how things are going at your house. I love you so much, Melissa, my wonderful daughter, my gift from God. I miss you. Give Shawn a big hug from his mama---and I will see you all one of these days.

Always in my heart,
Your Mommy


*************************************
12/07/12

Hi My Wonderful Daughter,
I want to pick up the phone and tell you about the neat Christmas decorations I saw in the store today. And I want to tell you about looking for things for your 3 precious kids, and how it broke my heart that you aren't here to share all the things we usually share during this season. Today I listened to Sandy Patti sing "our" song "The Gift goes On"---Remember when you, Summer and I sang that together? Every time I hear that I think of how much fun we had singing that together. The gift that God gave me in having you as a daughter goes on in all of my memories.

*How grateful I am to Him that He blessed me with you 33 years ago. I could sit here and write things like "Why"-------but that doesn't help. God gives me peace in knowing that you are so happy and complete in Him in heaven. Often I look at pictures of you and Shawn, and just want a glimpse of "your world" with God in person. How amazing you must feel--to look into the face of Jesus. I can't wait to join you someday. But I just miss you so much, and wanted you to know.*

*I love you, Melissa Anne. You will always be my little girl.*

*Love,*
*Mom*

\*\*\*\*\*\*\*\*\*\*\*\*\*\*\*\*\*\*\*\*\*\*\*\*\*\*\*\*\*\*\*\*\*\*\*\*\*\*\*\*

*6/6/2013*

Dear Melissa,
*I wish I could sit down and talk to you today. It's been almost a year now since you have been in heaven. Oh Melissa, you will always be my little girl. I have so many questions, but they really don't matter because the answers won't change the fact that you are not here. I am thinking so much about your kids, especially Jackson since he will turn 8 this week. Remember when we saw him on the ultrasound with you and Steve? He was kicking his little legs, and he had the hiccups. You were so excited to know you were going to be a mommy. You had looked forward to that for so many years. Memories---pictures--videos--that's what I have left here on earth. You existed.*

*You were my sweet, precious baby girl. I'll never forget when you were born. I wanted a girl so much. I loved my 4 boys with everything a mommy could love them with. But you filled a big hole in my heart because you were my daughter. Didn't we just have the best time sharing life? I just miss you so much. I felt like you were here today--so we had a little talk. Sometimes I do that, and it helps the pain, to some degree.*

———

*Anyway, I know you are content and perfect and satisfied in heaven----we talked often about what it would be like. I wouldn't ask you to come back because you would have to give up being in the very presence of Jesus, our precious Savior. Oh I just can hardly wait to look at him "Face to Face". Someday soon we will be together. Then I won't cry these tears of sadness and grief.*

*I know you are with Shawn, and my heart aches for him, too. I saw a helicopter today, looked up, and just wished that he would be the pilot---I wanted him back, too. But I know that you are there together, along with so many others. You have met your little brother or sister---the one I lost after Mickey. I never knew what it was, but you know. You can introduce me when I arrive. My heart broke when I lost that baby, and I never even got to raise him. I truly am grateful to God that He allowed me to raise you and Shawn, and that you lived some of your adult lives before you joined the saints in heaven.*

*I won't ask why now----like I said, it doesn't matter because it won't bring you back. But I love you, sweetheart, and will always be thankful that you did hear me tell you 2 times while you were in the hospital that I love you. You carried those words from me to heaven with you----I will always love you.*

*So I will say goodbye for now, and pray for your kids and Steve. They miss you, too, and I wonder if you can ever look down and see them. So many things to wonder about. Thank God for His promise that we will be together forever with Him. I can't wait!!*

*I LOVE YOU AND MISS YOU.*
My love forever and ever,
Mom

*********************************

7/5/2013

Hi Sweet Melissa,

*Who would have known that as I wrote to you a year ago today, July 5, 2012, that you wouldn't live much longer? Steve had called me on the evening of the 4th, and I got to talk to you to tell you to hang on, and tell you I love you. Even now this whole year is very difficult for me to believe. You did hang on for a couple of days, but as we were flying out to see you on July 8, 2012, Jesus enfolded you in His arms and transported you to heaven. I didn't get to see you alive; but I did get to cradle your body in my arms, find your temples were still warm, and try to let you go. I will never forget your body lying still, cold and lifeless. No mother could ever imagine a worse nightmare than losing a child--no matter how old.*

*First, 6 weeks earlier, we had said goodbye to Shawn---your 34 year old brother. And now, you too??? My questions keep me awake--I will never understand. But I know for a fact that you and Shawn are with Jesus and that does comfort me. I have to admit I'm more than a little jealous. You are experiencing everything that we live for. I could never ask you to come back. Selfishly I would in a heartbeat, but I know that you and Shawn are perfect and happy now. No more sadness. I just cannot wait to see you in heaven with Jesus, and the rest of our loved ones. Someday soon.*

*Meanwhile, God isn't finished with us here on earth. Your brothers and sister miss you and none of us know exactly how to handle our "smaller sized" family. But God's promises are true--so much to say about that.*

*Anyway, I just wanted to tell you that I love you and miss you more than you will ever know. I know I will write soon again and eventually be able to express everything I am feeling.*

*I love you, my wonderful, heavenly daughter. You are one of my greatest gifts on this earth!! I miss you so!!!*

*Love always and forever, Mom*

*******************************************

7/14/2013

*Well, Melissa, here it is----your funeral day plus one year. I woke up very early this morning thinking about you, the sadness I feel because you're not here, and just realizing the reality of the truth that I won't see you again until I go to heaven, too. I miss you, my sweet daughter. The tears just kept coming as I stayed in bed, so I finally just got up and tried to write to you. But the words wouldn't come then. Sometimes it just takes awhile to be able to go on thru the day----my human feelings are hard to overcome at times. But then, God must put me on someone's heart because all of a sudden I have His strength to help me, and I won't know where it came from. I don't always have the capacity to pray, so God asks someone else to help me out. And once again I feel hope, joy that you're actually with Jesus, and anticipation in knowing that "I Shall See You Soon Again" (love that song--it makes me cry). I have new pictures of your 3 kids, and*

*I know that they are getting thru with lots of help. I know Steve is getting thru with lots of help. You will always be my daughter--you were the "desire of my heart"!! I prayed for years that I would have a daughter because I had some wonderful boys already. I still know how blessed I am that you were given to me---I will always be thankful for you. So as you continue to enjoy the wonders of heaven that we won't know until we arrive, I will cherish the memories I have of you and look forward to reuniting when it's my time to join you. I love you so much and always will.*

*Bye for now, sweet girl.*
*Love, Mom*

\*\*\*\*\*\*\*\*\*\*\*\*\*\*\*\*\*\*\*\*\*\*\*\*\*\*\*\*\*\*\*\*\*\*\*\*\*\*\*\*\*\*\*

Shawn and Melissa's entrance into Heaven brought back to mind some wonderful experiences that occurred when my own Dad died years earlier. Shortly after his death Ginny and I were at the airport waiting for the arrival of one of the kids.

I was taken with a family who was anxiously awaiting the arrival of a loved one. They were standing on their tiptoes trying to get a glimpse of the first sighting. Then their loved one walked through the door – the hugs and the tears of joy were something to see.

I said to Ginny, "One of these days I am going to die. When I do, Jesus is going to tell my Dad that I am on my way and about ready to arrive. He will be standing on his tiptoes trying to get a glimpse of me when I walk through Heaven's door. And when I do, we are going to hug and cry. Boy that will be a reunion."

Now we knew that there would be two of our children waiting for our arrival too.

I also thought of an experience that happened to me while I was riding the bike paths in a park near the Des Moines River. As I peddled down the trail, I heard voices and music and laughter. I could not tell where this was coming from, but it sounded like these people were really having a grand time.

When I stopped and listened, I finally realized that it was a group of people just on the other side of the river. They were the ones who were having such a good time together. I could not see them, but I could hear them. They were just out of sight. The sound of their fellowship made you want to be there with them.

I remember how it struck me, "This is so similar to Heaven. My Dad did not leave the party – he is where the party is taking place! Heaven is just over the river. It is not far from here. I can almost hear the noise of the party!"

Yes, the concept of heaven was very real to us before, but now that we had two recent investments there, we developed an even greater interest in it. And that interest in Heaven helped us make it through the lonely days and nights.

## 4. The People God Sent Our Way

God is a Person, and as such, develops a personal relationship with us, His children. But He also sends people our way to be a "substitute" for Himself to provide a kind of comfort and healing that can only come in a "flesh and blood" format.

We are so thankful for the people who have come alongside us to help us. As soon as some heard the tragic news, they came to our home. Some cried with us, some prayed with us, some read Scripture to us, some brought food, and others just sat quietly and mourned with us.

Some, guessing that there must have been extreme costs to flying to Virginia and staying for a week in motels, sent cards with money. They would tell us that God laid it on their hearts to help us in a tangible way. It was a bit overwhelming to see that within the course of six weeks, God supplied, through people, the almost exact amount of expenses we had incurred.

I did not know, as I was writing the last paragraph, that God was planning on surprising us with a check in the mail. We had just returned from an unscheduled trip to Las Vegas to help to one of our kids who was struggling with the events of the last year and had incurred unexpected expenses. In the mail today, was a $1200 check from a long-time business friend in San Diego. He had not known about our need, but felt that God wanted him to send us some money.
Thank You, Father.

———

Many of Ginny's little piano students stopped by the house with their parents to give her a hug and convey their sympathy. You could see the sorrow and compassion in the eyes of the older children. It meant so much to Ginny.

Some of the kids decorated a number of flowerpots and planted flowers to serve as a memorial. We surrounded the tree in our yard with these and watered them all summer.

One of things of which we took note was that none of these people tried to provide the answers as to "why." I am guessing that with two suicides in six weeks, none of them were any better at explanations than we were. None of them came with religious platitudes and worn-out expressions – they just came to tell us they cared.

We believe we may have a better understanding now as to how to help hurting people that God brings into our life. The best help is an honest "I don't have the answers but my heart hurts for you."

The best definition of sympathy I have ever heard is "Your pain in my heart." That's all we need to convey to those who hurt. A listening ear, some time spent, a willingness to be available – not to supply all the answers.

True help was given to us by people who were willing to feel our pain and did not think they had to fix our pain.

## 5. The Past Memories We Shared

When I was just starting out in the ministry, I would visit the elderly people in my congregation. I learned something very quickly. It is good to talk to them about the past memories they have.

You see, we can have a tendency to avoid talking to them

about anything that we think might make them sad – like the past they no longer have. We assume it is inappropriate to discuss memories that make them wipe tears from their eyes.

Just the opposite is true. Discussing those past memories, under the cautious leading of the Holy Spirit, can be a real healing agent for them. Tears are not always bad for us.

We find that the past memories often remind us of something that makes us laugh – and that is good for us. It is helpful for us to talk with people who can tell us about their involvement with the kids. Some of these people were friends, others were teachers. They all add a type of healing to our hearts.

As time went on, we found ourselves looking at old pictures or old videos. These were especially helpful when shared together with our other kids. A "remember when" or an "I remember" would add details that we had forgotten, or in some cases that we had never known.

## 6. The Poignant Songs We Heard

Music has always been a big part of our lives. Music is playing in our home almost all of the time, especially Christian music. It played such a major role in helping us cope with the difficult days.

Christian music has been called "portable doctrine" because its Biblical teaching is "packaged" in such a way that you can carry it around in your head and heart all day long. If based on Biblical truth, the benefit of a song can be much more than something that appeals to our emotions.

I think it was the songwriting legend, Bill Gaither who said, "Our hearts are like the desert, and the music is the rain." That is how we felt so often – like the desert. Music was like a drink of cool, refreshing water to our souls.

We found that old familiar songs took on new meaning for us after the death of our kids. At times, it is like we were hearing the words of the song for the first time. We agreed with its truth before, but now we were relying on its truth to help us through the day.

How exactly did the songs help us? It was more than providing a distracting melody to get our minds off the kids. The songs seemed to address the needs of the moment. We often felt that God put us in "the right place at the right time" to hear the message of a specific song.

Here are a few of the specific areas of need the songs addressed.

**Comfort.** There were days when the greatest need we had was to feel the comforting presence of God. We needed to be reminded how much God cared about our tears. We needed to be reminded that everything is not "out of control" because God is in control.

I remember watching a Gaither Homecoming show on TV, and hearing Mark Lowry sing the old hymn, "Does Jesus Care?" I had heard that song dozens of times before, but this time, I really "heard" what it said.

*"Does Jesus care when my heart is pained too deeply for mirth and song: As the burdens press and the cares distress, and the way grows weary and long?" Does Jesus care when I've said 'good-bye' to the dearest on earth to me, And my sad heart aches til it nearly breaks – Is it aught to Him? Does He care?*

*O yes, He cares – I know He cares, His heart is touched with my grief; When the days are weary, the long nights dreary, I know my Savior cares."* (Words: Folliott S. Pierpoint, Music: Conrad Kocher, adapt. William Henry Monk)

You could sense that he was singing more than just words. He was sharing what he, himself, had experienced and found to be true. It really ministered to us.

*Conflict.* Several songs we listened to speak about the conflict that we experience – the conflict between wanting our loved ones back, and knowing it is best for them to stay where they are.

These songs remind us of the peace and joy that our children now have in Heaven, and how they are made perfectly whole. For them, all inner conflicts are over. In a tender way, the songs remind us that what would be "best" for us, to have them back, would not be "best" for them.

*Praise.* I previously shared with you how God drew our attention to a song that used the phrase, "God inhabits praise," and how the truth of that statement made such a difference to us.

There were other songs that reminded us of another truth about praise. That is the truth that it is one thing to praise God in the good times, but a far different thing to praise Him in the bad times.

I remember one song specifically that talked about Paul and Silas singing songs of praise to God while they were prisoners in a jail cell. Their singing in such adverse conditions made a spiritual impact on the other prisoners (Acts 16).

The song encouraged us to offer praise to God when the days became difficult. We found that doing so would quickly change our attitude. In other words our praise produced grateful hearts, which in turn produced a more positive perspective.

———

We think that offering God our song of praise in the midst of our problems was something that He used to "stretch our spiritual muscles." After all, a mark of maturity is being able to see the benefits that hard times produces in one's life.

*Perspective.* Other songs made us realize that there were two perspectives about our present circumstances- our perspective and God's perspective. One song became especially helpful as it reminded us that the Shepherd views our circumstances from the mountaintop, while we view them while in the valley.

It made us realize that our earthly perspective is very limited. So we chose to trust God and His perspective because it was so much more accurate than ours. That truth often encouraged us to keep us going.

*Hope.* Hope is the key ingredient that music brought to us on a daily basis. The melodies we hummed throughout the day were constant reminders to us that our hope for today and tomorrow rested in the faithfulness of our Heavenly Father. These songs reaffirmed the truth of Hebrews 6:19, "We have this hope as an anchor for the soul, firm and secure."

To be sure, God used poignant songs to minister to us hope; hope that was steadfast and sure because it was anchored, not in the circumstances around us, but in Heaven.

## 7. The Promises God Gives Us

I recorded over 40 specific promises that God gave us saying He would care for us and provide for our needs. But let me mention the most specific promise He gave us was at the very beginning of the cycle of our losses in July 2011.

This promise was 1 Samuel 30 about David at Ziklag. One day God revealed an entirely new truth I had not seen before although I had read the passage dozens of times. I used bold type to emphasize the words that "jumped off the page" that morning.

*"And it came to pass, when David and his men were come to Ziklag on the third day, that the Amalekites had invaded the south, and Ziklag, and smitten Ziklag, and burned it with fire; And had taken the women captives, that were therein: they slew not any, either great or small, but carried them away, and went on their way. So David and his men came to the city, and, behold, it was burned with fire; and their wives, and their **sons**, and their **daughters**, were taken captives."*

*"Then David and the people that were with him lifted up their voice and wept, until they had no more power to weep. And David's two wives were taken captives, Ahinoam the Jezreelitess, and Abigail the wife of Nabal the Carmelite. And David was greatly distressed; for the people spake of stoning him, because the soul of all the people was grieved, every man for his **sons** and for his **daughters**: but David encouraged himself in the LORD his God. "*

*"And David said to Abiathar the priest, Ahimelech's son, I pray thee, bring me hither the ephod. And Abiathar brought thither the ephod to David. And David enquired at the LORD, saying, Shall I pursue after this troop? Shall I overtake them? And he answered him, Pursue: for thou shalt surely overtake them, and without fail recover all."*
*"And David recovered all that the Amalekites had carried away: and David rescued his two wives. And there was nothing lacking to them, neither small nor great, neither **sons** nor **daughters**, neither spoil, nor any thing that they had taken to them: David recovered all."*

I was reminded of what God had shared with me from these

verses previously:

**1.** David lost everything he had - family, finances, future (1-2)

**2.** David was beyond himself with grief due to what he has lost (v. 6a)

**3.** David found encouragement in the Lord his God (v. 6b)

**4.** David sought wisdom from God as to what he should do (vs. 7-8)

**5.** David was told to pursue after those who had robbed him (v. 8)

**6.** David was promised that even though he was greatly outnumbered, God would restore everything that had been taken from him (v. 8)

**7.** David recovered all he had lost (v.18)

Now, I saw for the first time that the grief of 1 Samuel 30 was focused on the loss of his family members– specifically, their **sons and daughters**: *"Because the soul of all the people was grieved, every man for his **sons and for his daughters**"* (verse 6).

This phrase is mentioned three separate times in this passage! I saw for the first time that God's comforting promise to us that we would "recover all," applied to the unjust loss of a job, but more importantly to the unexpected **loss of our two kids – our son and daughter.**

## DOUBLE APPLICATION. Therefore, the story of Ziklag had a double application for us. We leaned on God's promise of "recovering all" when I lost my job, but that was just the precursor to losing our children.

———

We did not know what "recovering all" meant in detail, but the promise said to us, "You don't have to worry about things. I know what has happened to you, and I am in control. I have you in the palm of My hand, and until the day when I right all the wrongs, I will take care of you. Your responsibility is just to trust Me."

You see, one of these days Ginny and I will "recover" all our losses! In that day all the wrongs will be righted, and all the losses will be replaced. We will have abundantly more than we had before!

We have God's promise of a reunion with our kids and an eternal restitution. ***The loss is for now; the gain will be forever.***

God will be Debtor to no man. He never takes away but what He replaces, and restores, and returns more than He has taken. Job 42:10 tells us that *"the Lord gave Job twice as much as he had before."* God gives, He takes, and He gives again. In the final chapter of the book God's giving is always more than His taking.

Sometimes His restitution to us occurs in this life, and at other times in the next life. Sometimes the return is in material things, and sometimes the return is in immaterial things. God decides all those details, and all He asks of us is to trust Him.

What a God! A God that is so involved in our lives that He can supernaturally lead us to a promise in His Word, then re-emphasize that promise with late night TV preachers, black Gospel singers, 150-year-old devotionals, Sunday afternoon TV shows, a young man in the financial field whose pastor has just preached on Ziklag the Sunday before, and the mother of two new piano students who couldn't wait to tell us about the message concerning Ziklag that she had heard that morning in church!

I believe that a God who exerts that much effort and energy to impress upon my dull mind a 4000 year-old story about the city of Ziklag, must be worthy of my trust, my devotion, and my service.

———

# Part Seven

*Blessings Disguised As*
*Impossible Situations*

August of 2013 was a big month! We were scheduled to take depositions from my former boss, the HR Director, and several of the employees. I was somewhat anxious to see how this lawsuit was going to play out. I was especially curious to see what explanations would be given for my firing other than my age and health which is what we were contending.

It had now been two full years now since events went into motion that took our lives from "cruise control" to "out of control." It seemed to us that few areas were left unchanged – our finances, our health, our plans for the future, our daily routines, and especially our relationship with God.

Three events occurred in August that some would call "bad luck." Looking back, they were actually God's blessings in disguise.

### The First "Blessing"
### *Pain*

"Duck! – Here Comes Your Own Advice!" Have you ever given someone advice, then later on, something happens that seems like God is saying to you, "That was really great advice you gave a while back – now I am going to give you an opportunity to live your advice in your own life."

Months earlier, I had a conversation with one of my sons about a statement made by Dr. Charles Swindoll, "Some of God's choicest blessings can come disguised as impossible situations." In other words, it is easy to see how a new car can be a blessing from God, but how about a car accident?

We talked about Jacob in the Old Testament, the guy who wrestled all night with the angel. You recall that Jacob was clinging to the Angel and would not let him go until he promised to bless Jacob (Genesis 32). The blessing Jacob received came in two parts: (1) God changed his name to "Israel" which means "God rules," and (2) God touched the "hollow of Jacob's thigh" and put his hip out of place.

The new name was not so bad - every time "Israel" was spoken, Jacob was reminded to trust in God instead of himself, but the new "pain" was not so enjoyable - every step Jacob took hurt! That pain was also to remind him to rely on God.

Both the new name and the new pain gave Jacob a better vantage point to listen to the voice of God. But we concluded that the pain was probably the more effective reminder to Jacob than was the new name.

The "pain" God sends our way could be in our bodies, or it could be in our hearts – both are effective. We decided in our chat that we should expect God to bless us with "pain" occasionally, in order to give us a better vantage point to listen to His voice.

C.S. Lewis said pain is "God's megaphone." In the midst of it, we can hear God whisper to us, or we can hear Him shouting to us. Either way, pain affords us an opportunity to hear God in a different way.

I was reminded of that conversation, when during the first part of August, I developed a herniated disk and a resulting hip problem. The only relief from excruciating pain I could find was to lie on my side in the bed with ice. That is what I did for three entire weeks.

Being bedfast gave me some time to think – that's about all I could do – lay and think. At first, I thanked God for sending the physical problem, but before long I found it difficult to be thankful.

I finally prayed, "God, I thank you for your blessings, but is there any way you could stop blessing me so much? I am really tired of this!" Do I have to tell you that, even after two years of God refining my faith, I saw how very far I have to go in this area.

Sharing advice is easy to do, but living that advice is a different story! The pain was the first in a series of three events that came in rapid succession. I would categorize all three events as blessings of God – but they were "disguised as impossible situations."

### The Second "Blessing"
### Loss of Income

The second event – or "blessing" - that occurred in August had to do with the loss of one of our income flows. Shortly after my termination, I had been asked to work as a consultant for a non-profit organization.

In August, the Director of the organization notified me that the group just did not have enough money to continue partnering with me.

That may not seem like a big deal, but that lack of sponsorship meant two things to us: (1) I could no longer do what I loved to do – teach young people how to become financially savvy, and (2) I would no longer have that additional income.

The back pain, the medication, and now the loss of one of our few income sources seemed to put a "magnifying glass" on what God was asking us to readily accept.

I recall saying to my wife one day, "Honey, is it just me, or does it seem to you, too, that God is continuing to remove the sources of our security, one-by-one? I know He is behind the scenes working things out, but sometimes it gets pretty scary!"

It made me realize that it does not take major losses to push us in the direction of discouragement; the small ones, especially if they are prolonged, can do the very same thing.

### The Third "Blessing"
## Not Winning Our Court Case

The result of the depositions would be the third event that would fit into the category of disguised blessings. I was under the impression that my case would be won if my boss would admit on record that he had talked about my age and my poor health when he fired me. I found out that this was not the case.

He readily admitted that he had mentioned both my age and health when he fired me. But he offered a much different explanation for his words (I will paraphrase): "I did mention to Jim that he was going to be 62, and I did mention that he was not in good health, but the reason I did so was to make sure he realized that, not having much to offer the market place, he should be extremely grateful to me for allowing him to work as an independent contractor." (paraphrase)

Then he explained his reason for terminating me: "Jim was fired because I found out that he was charging me a profit for a booklet I had been buying from him. He wrote it, but my company owned it. He had no business making a profit on a booklet I owned!"

"When I confronted Jim about this, he knew he was guilty! Then he returned the profit from the last order, which was absolute proof that he knew he had been caught red-handed." (paraphrase)

Before the depositions were ended, my attorney said to me, "I have never had a case go downhill so quickly!" She explained: **(1)** the first statement gave the jury an alternate explanation for mentioning of my age and health, and **(2)** his second statement gave the jury a reason other than my age or health for termination.

She went on to explain that it did not matter if what my boss believed at the time of termination was true or not; it only mattered that, at the time, he believed it to be true. The fact that he thought he owned the booklets provided an alternative reason for my firing other than the reason of age or health.

So, if he had fired me because he thought I was Jesse James - that was a different reason other than age or health. It did not matter that he was mistaken as to who I was, it only mattered what he believed to be true.

Or if he fired me because he thought I was an alien from Mars - that too would be a different reason for firing other than age or health. The facts of his belief are not relevant; only that he actually believed those things to be true.

So, even though my boss later admitted on record that he had indeed been mistaken about who owned the booklets, it made no difference in my case. His mistaken belief was still a reason for firing me other than my age or health.

If the jury could be given any other plausible reason for my termination, other than age or health, I had a good chance of losing. It would cost us an additional $7-10 thousand dollars to proceed with a court trial, so we decided to settle out of court.

I cannot tell you about the settlement agreement, but I can tell you that God did just what He promised He would do. He promised me in 1 Samuel 30, "Pursue, and everything that was taken from you will be recovered." We recovered everything that was taken from us at the time I was terminated – no more, no less.

———

Looking back, we have no regrets. We had sought God's direction in the matter, and were convinced that He led us to file a discrimination suit. He said "Pursue," and we did. We left the rest up to Him.

———

# Part Eight

## Why?

## The Questions Begin

In the weeks that followed the settlement, I became aware of a certain word that kept creeping into my thoughts – "Why?"

When I had argued with God back in July of 2011 about giving the profit back to my boss, why did He tell me, "I take care of you, not your boss"? Didn't He know that giving the profit back would be perceived as an admission of guilt?

Why had He allowed me to be fired unjustly? Why had He allowed my friends and co-workers to believe I had done something wrong, when I had not? Why was there no way for me to show the world that a grave injustice had been done?

And why did He lead us to file a lawsuit if He knew we were not going to win it in court? Why was there not a great big settlement so we could use it the rest of our lives?

Why was I forced out of job that I loved? Why were we now living on partial Social Security, and why did He think it was a good idea to remove another source of our income?

Why did He let our two children take their own lives? Why didn't He stop them? Why did our daughter die before we were able to get to her? And why did my wife have to suffer so?

Why was it necessary to endure such pain and sorrow? Why, in the midst of all this stress, did He think it was a great time to put me bed for three weeks with constant pain?

And why did He ask me to write this book? Why did God so drastically have to change our lives – we were doing okay like we were – why make life so hard?

## Why? Why? Why? Why? Why?

Once I began to ask why, the whys had to "stand in line,"

---

because I had a whole bunch of them!

While a freshman in Bible College, I heard a traveling Evangelist say from the pulpit, "We should never ask God 'Why?' It is a sin to ask God 'Why?'"

I thought long and hard about those statements. Is that really true? Is it wrong to ask why? I decided to go to the Scripture to see if it had any information about asking God "Why?"

God led me to this passage: *"And about the ninth hour, Jesus cried with a loud voice, saying, Eli, Eli, lama sabachthani, that is to say, My God, My God, why hast thou forsaken me?"* Matthew 27:46

Jesus was quoting a thousand year-old prophecy from Psalm 22:1 *"Why hast Thou forsaken me? Why art Thou so far from helping me?"* This verse predicted that Christ would ask *"why"* the Father was forsaking Him while He hung on the cross in the place of the sinner.

Verse 1 predicts the question, verse 3 provides the answer: *"Thou art holy."* The Holy Father forsook His Son when His Son took upon Himself the punishment for the sins of the world. God forsaken of God – a concept beyond my ability to grasp!

Jesus asked His Father *"Why?"* That means it cannot be a sin to ask God why! It cannot be unbelief. It cannot be wrong!

I concluded that God is not upset with His child when asked "why?" If Jesus Christ asked "why," we are in pretty good company when we do the same.

"Why" is the cry of the human heart for answers, and it is not wrong to seek answers. God is not offended by our questions. Our questions are not always answered, but they are always welcome.

I am convinced that the answers to the question "Why?" will lead us to fear, or they will lead us to faith. But how do we go about getting the answers to "why?"

Maybe a good starting point would be to list some of the things we learned from the experience. If someone asks you why you took a four-week class on photography, your answer might include what you "learned" from the class.

Similarly, after being a student in "God's classroom," some of the "whys" might be answered by thinking about what was learned.

The Psalmist said, *"It is good for me that I have been afflicted, that I might learn thy statutes"* ( Psalm 119:71). Learning about God resulted from the affliction.

1 Peter 1:6 adds, *"In this ye greatly rejoice, though now for a season, if needs be, ye are in heaviness through manifold trials."* It is God Who determines the training is necessary.

These verses make me think of that old TV commercial for some aftershave lotion. You know the one where the guy, after shaving, is slapped in the face and responds, "Thanks, I needed that!"

Our Heavenly Father knows what we need to learn about Him in order to be able to serve Him better and love Him more, and He knows what it will take to cultivate that knowledge in us. Again I remind you that God does not give us a "vote" in the matter because He determines the training that is a "necessity!" If we had a choice, we would always choose the easier path – even though it affords fewer opportunities for learning.

———

So, God is at the very center of our suffering. He will never allow the fire to get too hot, nor will He allow us to stay in the furnace (classroom) too long.

Having said all that, what lessons or knowledge did we learn about God from the last two years that might help us answer "why?"

I am going to list five lessons, but understand as I do that, (1) I am not saying we have learned all there is to learn about the matter – we are not great students; and (2) the lessons are not listed in their order of importance.

### Lesson One
### Everything God Does Is For Our Good And His Glory

*For Our Good.* Most Christians have committed to memory Romans 8:28: "And we know that all things work together for good to them that love God, to them who are the called according to his purpose."

Stop and think a minute what this verse is saying. It is saying that God is able to take "all things" (every experience of life) and in some way use it for our good. To believe that truth in the midst of "bad times" can be a sustaining force, especially when "the things" that are happening are so bad we cannot see how any good could ever occur.

I like what Philip Yancy wrote in his book Disappointment With God *"Not until history has run its course will we understand how 'all things work together for good.' Faith means believing in advance what will only make sense in reverse."* (to order Zondervan. http://zondervan.com/9780310517818)

Looking back over the last years, Ginny and I have become different people. God has done something inside. To be sure, we are still just a couple of sinners saved by grace, but our perspective about God, about life, about ourselves, and about our future has been forever changed. We seem to be a bit more "focused" on the fact that God is in control of our lives, and deserves to be trusted.

Let's face it – either God knows what He is doing or He doesn't. Isn't that the essence of trusting Him? He is trustworthy when we can explain it, and He is trustworthy when we cannot explain it.

We chose to believe the words that Dr. R.T. Ketcham had penned in the midst of severe trials decades ago: "God is too loving to be unkind and too wise to make mistakes." Wow! What an insight!

Dr. Ketcham is also noted for saying, "*The only thing I have to give to God is my obedience.*" (Portrait of Obedience. RegularBaptistPress.org) Sounds like he was a man that had learned something from hard times.

*For His Glory.* God gave me a promise early on that I held on to with both hands: "*That they may know that this is Thy hand, that Thou, Lord, hast done it.*" (Psalm 109:27) I did not fully understand that promise then, nor do I understand it fully today, but I know that it means at least this – what was taking place in our lives is somehow going to bring God glory.

When I was in Bible College in the early seventies, I read an interview in Times Magazine with Dr. Jack Hyles, Pastor of First Baptist Church in Hammond, Indiana. He was asked to explain how, with his simple upbringing in East Texas, he had built a church that was averaging over 26,000 per Sunday.

His answer was so insightful, it has stayed with me all these years: "The best I can explain that to you is that God looked down from Heaven and said, 'I need to find the most crooked old stick I can find. I am going to do a great and marvelous work with that stick. When I am done, everybody will know that I accomplished the work, not the stick."

From the very onset of losing my job at age 61, I felt that this verse was telling me that God was executing a plan that would eventually bring honor and glory to Him. I actually do not know any of the details that are involved in the fulfillment of this promise, but I know that one of the outcomes will be that God is going to get the credit for it in a very unique way.

This is surely in keeping with what Jesus taught his disciples about the sickness and subsequent death of Lazarus in John 11, *"This sickness is…for the glory of God, that the Son of God might be glorified by it."*

Were the things that happened to Lazarus for his good? Yes. But the events surrounding the life, death, and resurrection of Lazarus also occurred for the glory of God.

If you believe, as I do, that the will of God is usually understood only when it is history, you do not have to worry about how God is going to bring it all about. That is His part; my part is to trust Him.

*For Others.* Let me point out one last thing about this promise that God gave me from Psalm 102, *"That they may know that this is Thy hand, that Thou, Lord, hast done it."*

Do you notice that the promise specifically says, "that they may know that this is Thy hand" Who is the "they" that is being talked about here? Frankly, I have no idea, but I know that there are other people who will in someway learn what God is able to do and be to His own, by hearing what He did for us.

So the things that happened to us occurred for the benefit of other people too? Yes. I do not know who they are or how

———

they will find out about the events we experienced over the last couple of years, but when they do, they will have a better understanding of God's love and care for His children.

## *Lesson Two*
### *Life Can Be Planned, Not Controlled*

Ginny and I had done a certain amount of planning, specifically when it came to our finances. We wanted to become debt free, and we followed a plan to do so. We did not live life like beggars, but we were cautious with our spending in order to pay off our cars, then make double house payments. Our planning paid off, and in September of 2008 we became totally debt free.

So, here we were in our "golden years," growing old together and enjoying life. We had no debt, our needs were met, and things were peaceful. We loved each other, and we loved our family. Each year, it seemed another one of the kids would present us with another precious grandchild. Life was good.

Then, out of the blue, August 1, 2011, occurred, and life started to change. The peace we had known was replaced with confusion and chaos. And while we were trying to work through my 2011 August job loss, our son committed suicide on May 24, 2012. Still dazed and reeling from that awful tragedy, our daughter took her life on July 8, 2012.

It would be fair to say that by July 9th, 2012, no one needed to convince us that we were not in control! In fact, the circumstances all around us screamed to us in a deafening voice, "Everything is out of control!"

All of our planning, all of our praying, even the way we had raised our children seemed to no avail! None of it mattered in the outcome. Nothing we had done or could do seemed to have any affect on the downward spiral of life. We were absolutely, positively powerless. We had control over nothing!

———

One thing that resulted from being in this helpless state is that we started to learn just how much we are not in control of life. It is ok to have goals and plans, but we shouldn't be too shocked when God steps in and changes them. After all, the will of God is not God putting His blessing on our plans. The will of God is God drawing up the plans for our lives all by Himself!

When my daughter, Rachel, was just a toddler we were leaving the house for church one slick Iowa wintry night. As we left the doorway of the house, Rachel lifted up her little hand and wrapped it around my two fingers.

After I saw how slick it was, I bent over and carefully released her grip from my fingers. She started to fuss. I then took her little hand and put it in mine. No longer was her safety dependent on her holding on to me. Oh no, now her safety was dependent upon me holding on to her.

Oh, my friend, it is so hard to see when our eyes are filled with tears and our hearts are breaking, that God is in the process of "releasing our grip."

He is doing this so that He can be in control and hold on to us. The path ahead is too treacherous, and our grip is not strong enough to keep us secure. He must release our grip so He can hold us securely in His grip. The path just ahead is far too treacherous for us to hold on to Him – He must hold on to us!

So, when our best-laid plans in life are thrown aside, and life seems out of control, it may be that God is in the process of "changing grips." The path ahead requires God's grip to keep us secure. He must change places with us and sit in the Captain's seat.

Turbulent times often call for a change "in grips."

———

*Lesson Three*
## God Is Preparing Us For What He Is Preparing Us For

We are not to live in the past, but we are to learn from the past. That's one of the reasons why you will find the word "remember" used over 150 times in the Bible. We are to "remember" the past and how God brought calmness to the chaos, solace to storm, and peace to the problem. Reflecting upon His faithfulness, His tenderness, His love, and His goodness to us affects our perspective about the present situation and the future.

Remembering the past plays another role in helping us through difficulties because it seems to help us "connect the dots." We look back and can begin to see a plan that God was orchestrating behind the scenes. He was using people, circumstances, and events, to prepare us for what He was preparing us for.

At the beginning the promises God gave me from 1 Samuel 30 about Ziklag were totally focused on my job loss. If that were their only purpose, I am eternally grateful for how they got me through that difficult time. And for Him to remind me in so many different ways and times, that as He took care of David, He would take care of me, was such a blessing.

During the ten months from my firing to the first suicide, we had became somewhat "accustomed" to trusting God in a way that we had not done before. Although I had preached for thirty years about how loving and trustworthy He is, I was able to experience these truths on a whole new level. The promises on the pages of God's Word were put into the "working clothes of everyday life."

Looking back from my present vantage point, I can see how the first loss was a preparation for the losses to come. All of those things that God had done for us during those first ten months served to show us that He would stay right beside us and help us through. God was proven to be faithful. What we learned from the first loss prepared us for the subsequent losses.

In fact, I see now that many of those precious promises that God gave me at the beginning became sweeter still as they became real all over again. The losses I was focused on from 1 Samuel 30 were the "things" that had been taken away from David. Later on, I saw that the greater losses of 1 Samuel 30 were their "sons and daughters." And so it turned out to be with us.

I also can see now that God had been preparing me for the events of 2011-2013 through the many years of pastoral ministry. The truths from the 30 years of messages I preached, thirty years of ministering to people in their heartache, and thirty years of studying God's Word – were all used by the Lord to sustain me now in the present.

Those lessons from the past were brought out, dusted off, and used to bless me all over again. I knew they were true before, but now I experientially knew they were true.

I guess the longer one lives, the more you can look back and draw from the things you have learned about God thus far. It is clear that those things in our past are, in some Divine way, being used to prepare us for what God is preparing us for.

Neither Ginny nor I know what the future holds for us, but we wonder if God has some new direction for our lives after having gone through the losses of the last couple of years? We believe that God is preparing us for a new chapter in our lives – but He has not chosen to share any details of that with us at the moment.

I am confident though, that in His own time, He will reveal to us step-by-step what He wants us to do to serve Him now. He will open doors that we could never open, and He will close doors so that we do not journey down the wrong path.

And as always, His part is to lead, our part is to trust Him.

It is exciting to think about it. We are not fearful. If God was faithful to us before, He will be faithful to us in the future.

*Lesson Four*
### God's Promises Are Only Words Until You Trust Them

The story is told of a missionary who was attempting to translate John's Gospel into the native language of the people to which he ministered. These people were a very deceptive and untrustworthy people, not known for their honesty and kindness.

The missionary was finding it extremely difficult to come up with a word in their language that meant "to trust, to believe, to have faith in." As he tried to translate John 3:16 "whosoever believes in Him," he just could not come up with words to express the meaning.

Near noon a little native boy entered his office to tell him it was time for his lunch. After delivering the message, the little boy sat down in the chair directly across from the missionary's desk. He sighed a big sigh and said, "How good it is to rest my whole weight on this chair!"

Hearing that statement, the missionary exclaimed, "That is it! That is how I will translate the word 'believe. For God so loved the world, that He gave his only begotten Son, that whoever rests their whole weight on Him, should not perish, but have everlasting life."

The promises of God are not true just because we happen to believe them. But the promises of God come alive when we are put in a position to have to trust them. When we "rest our whole weight " upon them, they become very real and precious to us.

They become God's promises to us specifically, not just to His children in general. As they meet us in personal application, we find experientially that those promises do not break when we stand on them!

They remain steadfast and sure as we rest our whole weight on their trustworthiness. They teach us that our Heavenly Father is just what He says He is – faithful.

Up until then, God's promises are only words. But when they are relied upon to sustain us, to give us peace, to give us hope, to get us through the darkest night and the longest day, they take on a whole new meaning to us.

After the last couple of years, dozens of promises from God's Word have taken on a very personal meaning to us. We held on to them with both hands in the times of our greatest need, and they sustained us.

We found 1 Kings 8:56 to be true, *"there hath not failed one word of all His good promise which He promised."*

### Lesson Five
### It is Okay To Not Have All The Answers

I am a person who has always asked "why," not about just spiritual things, but about life in general. Most of the time this type of thinking is acceptable, but what does one do when God places you in a series of events that you cannot figure out the "whys" or the "wherefores?"

In those times God teaches us that it is okay not to have all the answers. That does not mean there are no answers, but just that we are not privy to them – yet.

Another quote from Philip Yancy helped me realize this fact: *"Maybe one of the reasons that we remain ignorant of God's ways is, not because He enjoys keeping us in the dark, but because we do not have the faculties to absorb so much light."* (Disappointment With God (http://zondervan.com/9780310517818).

Could it be that if God decided to explain to us "why" He changed our life so drastically from being on "cruise control" to "spiraling down at breakneck speed," we still would not get it? That seems very possible to me.

Maybe the finite (us) should not expect to understand the Infinite (God)? Maybe that fact will bring us to the realization that He is God, alone, and we are not.

Isaiah 55:8-9 seems to establish this division pretty clearly between human and Divine:

*"For my thoughts are not your thoughts, neither are your ways my ways," declares the Lord. As the heavens are higher than the earth, so are my ways higher than your ways, and my thoughts than your thoughts."* (New International Version)

The Voice translates it this way, *"My intentions are not always yours, and I do not go about things as you do. My thoughts and My ways are above and beyond you, just as heaven is far from your reach here on earth."*

This must be what Matthew Henry, the great Bible expositor of yesteryear meant when he wrote, "When we cannot by searching find the bottom, we must sit down at the brink and adore the depth."

I imagine that most of us envision that day when in Heaven we rush up to Jesus and say, "I have waited so long to understand why you allowed this or that to happen while I lived on earth." Or as Ricky Ricardo, Lucy's husband, would have put it, "You got a lot of splainin' to do."

Maybe one day, when we have the ability to see things more like God sees them, God will explain our unanswered questions. I can see that Scripture allows room for such a thing.

Or there is another scenario that just might be what occurs. We may approach Jesus to get our earthly questions answered, but while we are waiting to talk to Him, we decide, "These questions just don't matter any more." We are at perfect and complete peace. Everything will be as it should be. Those "earth questions" are not important any longer.

I do not know if we will one day have all the answers given to us, or if one day our earthly questions will no longer matter. Either way, we will be satisfied with the knowledge that God knew exactly what He was doing with our lives on earth. He made no mistakes.

Ginny and I have a lot of unanswered questions, but we have decided, dear friend, that it is okay with us to not have all the answers. We have made the conscious choice to live with the unanswered questions and lay them at the feet of the Lord Jesus. He knows our questions and our hurting hearts. If in His grace, He decides to reveal some of the answers to us, fine. But if not, that is fine too.

Benjamin Malachi Franklin (1882-1965) wrote these beautiful words that, again, have been in the cover of my Bible for 25 years:

> *"My life is but a weaving between my Lord and me.*
> *I cannot choose the colors that He works steadily.*
> *Oft times He weaves sorrow, and I in foolish pride,*
> *Forget He sees the upper – but I the underside.*

———

*Not till the loom is silent,*
*And the shuttles cease to fly, (if even then)*
*Shall God unroll the canvas*
*And explain the reason why.*
*The dark threads were as needful*
*In the Weaver's skillful hand*
*As the threads of gold and silver*
*To weave the pattern He had planned."*

———

# CONCLUSION

## Who Will We Trust To Take Care of Us?

*"I take care of you, not your boss."* Those were the words that God whispered to my heart in the middle of a sleepless night in July 2011. They came as the answer to my prayer for direction, for comfort, for encouragement.

These words actually presented me with a choice – a choice of where I would place my trust. Would I trust God with my life, or would I place my trust in my own abilities?

Years ago I had trusted God with my eternity. I placed my faith in His Son, Jesus, to be my personal Savior and Sin-bearer. "But as many as received him, to them gave he power to become the sons of God, even to them that believe on his name" John 1:12

Having trusted Him with my eternity, it seems only right to trust Him with my life here on earth. After all, if He can "take care of me" as far as my eternity is concerned, He can certainly "take care of me" on my way there.

So, I made a choice that night to trust God when He said He would "take care of me." I had no way of knowing that my choice would set in motion a chain of events that forever would change our lives.

I see now that my choice gave God the "the green light" if you please, to begin a process of refining our faith. I am glad that we could not see the future at that time, because I did not have enough grace to handle what was coming until it came.

"Refining" is a word we do not use a lot in our conversations, but a word that has deep meaning in the Christian realm. It means "to reduce to a pure state, to purify, to make or become elegant or polished, to become free of impurities."

This process of refining our faith is mentioned numerous times in Scripture:

———

"That the trial of your faith, being much more precious than of gold that perishes, though it be tried with fire, might be found unto praise and honor and glory at the appearing of Jesus Christ." 1 Peter 1:7 (KJV)

*"See, I have refined you, though not as silver; I have tested you in the furnace of affliction"* (Isaiah 48:10); *"But he knows the way that I take; when he has tested me, I will come forth as gold"* (Job 23:10); *"For you, God, tested us; you refined us like silver"* (Psalm 66:10); *"I will refine them like silver and test them like gold"* (Zechariah 13:9).

Apparently, our faith is very important to God. It must be. You see, in the refining process, God lets His child suffer extreme hardship – in fact, He not only lets him, He causes him to suffer.

I am sure that Our Father's heart breaks as our hearts break during this process. The purpose is to produce a purer, stronger faith.

I read these interesting words about "real faith" on the website of apologist Dr. John Ankerberg (www.jas.org) penned by author Mrs. Nancy Missler. She was describing the faith that Abraham possessed and how he obeyed God against all visible and logical evidence.

*"Real faith is not feeling, not seeing, not understanding and not knowing. Real faith is being convinced that no matter what "we" see happening, no matter what we understand to be true, and no matter how we feel, God will be faithful to His Word and He will perform His promises to us, in His timing and in His way!"*

*"Real faith is allowing God to be God. It's allowing God to do in our lives all that He needs to do (good or bad from our point of view), in order to conform us into His image. Real faith is allowing God to*

*strip us, flay us and crucify us, if that's what is needed to purge and sanctify our soul from sin and self."*

*"True faith allows God to do all that He needs to do in order to make us holy so that we can dwell in and enjoy His presence. True faith accepts God's night seasons as part of His will towards us in order to accomplish His will in us. And, at the same time, faith clings to God's promises of a future 'new' day."* (Used by permission)

Wow! What an insight into the kind of faith that God wants to develop in our hearts.

I have thought a lot about those words, "I take care of you, not your boss." I have concluded that I am not the only one to whom God whispers those words. He whispers the same words to you, dear friend.

He is vitally concerned about us and in what or whom we will place our trust. Will we trust God, or will we trust some other source of reliance – some other "boss" if you please?

**First and foremost, will we trust Him with our eternity?** He has provided forgiveness for all our sins, past, present, and future, through His finished work on Calvary's cross. His provision of salvation becomes ours when, by simple faith, we ask Him to become our Savior and Sin-bearer.

Here's what He promises: *"For God so loved the world that he gave his one and only Son, that whoever believes in him (rests their whole weight on Him) shall not perish but have eternal life...to all who did receive him, to those who believed in his name, he gave the right to become children of God...For it is by grace you have been saved, through faith – and this is not from yourselves, it is the gift of God, not by works, so that no one can boast"* (John 3:16, 1:12, Ephesians 2: 8-9).

If you have never trusted Him with your eternity, would you right now confess to God that you are a sinner in need of His Son to be your Savior? Will you tell God that you are placing your faith and trust in what Jesus did for you on the Cross? The Bible promises, *"That whosoever call on the name of the Lord shall be saved."* Romans 10:13

There is no more urgent or important decision we can make. Where we spend eternity depends upon whether we have trusted Him as our personal Savior.

***Second, will we trust Him with our life here on earth?*** If He is able to save us from our sins, He is certainly able to keep us safe and secure through life's sunshine and storms. As His child, He promises that everything that happens will be to our ultimate good and His ultimate glory!

It is easier for us to see how much we need to trust God with our life when the storms of life knock us off our feet. Then we find it relatively easy to see our weakness and reach out for His strength.

Maybe this explains why He allows the storms to beset us – storms produce faith, sunshine does not! Problems purify us; prosperity does not!

Does that mean choosing God to "take care of you" will likely lead to times of problems and testing?

That does seem to be how it works. Even of Jesus it was written, *"Although He was a Son, He learned obedience from the things which He suffered."* Hebrews 5:8

So, you have to ask yourself, "If I choose to trust God, will it be worth it?"

I know of no one better to answer that question than the man

———

who's very name brings to mind the word "suffering" – Job. Did Job think that trusting God to take care of him was worth it?

Here's what Job concluded: *"He knoweth the way that I take; When he hath tried me, I shall come forth as gold...Though he slay me, yet will I trust in him..."* Job 23:10; 35:15. (KJV)

Life is difficult no matter which path we choose – with or without God. But with God there is peace in the problems, calmness in the chaos, and significance to the storms.

In this process of refining us, God assured us with repeated promises from Ziklag. He came along side us with God-Hugs at the very times when we needed to sense His presence the most. He sent precious people who stood in His place and ministered to us. He gave us songs that brought sunshine to our days and sleep to our sleepless nights.

He taught us spiritual lessons about Himself, about ourselves, about life, and about death that we had never learned before – at least not to that degree.

And He will take the whole process and somehow use it all to bring honor and glory to His name.

He has earned and deserves our trust. He said, "I will take care of you" and He has.

We don't understand it all, but we are in close contact with the One who does - AND THAT IS ENOUGH FOR NOW

## *About Jim and Ginny*

Jim and Ginny Garnett were both born and raised in the Mid-West, and were fortunate enough to have careers that utilized their God-given talents and abilities. Jim is a communicator and has served as a public speaker, author, educator, and counselor. Ginny's gifts lie in the areas of music and mothering, being an accomplished pianist, mother of six, grandmother of twenty+, and great-grandmother of one (so far).

Both were under the age of ten when with childlike faith they trusted Jesus as their Savior and Lord. Both are familiar with the life and ministry of a pastor's life and ministry with Ginny being born into a pastor's family making her a "PK" (preacher's kid). Jim served as a Senior Pastor for over 30 years.

In 2018 they moved from the Mid-west to beautiful Henderson, Nevada, where they are now retired.

**Jim and Ginny Garnett**
**Henderson, NV**

jimgarnettbooks@gmail.com

# Jim Garnett Books

## Books on Faith

**When Life Goes From Cruise Control To Out of Control.** This Mid-western couple suffered the loss of two adult children to suicide within six weeks of each other. They learned the answer to the question, "Where is God when the bottom drops out of life?" **ASIN: B00LYO1W30**

**The Prosperity Gospel – Gospel of Greed.** "The Prosperity Gospel offers people the same things the Devil offers to those who will worship him – they just do so in the name of Christ." John MacArthur
"The problem with the Prosperity Gospel is that prosperity is the gospel." John Piper **ASIN: B08KJ6696V**

## Books on Finance

**The Nuts and Bolts of Cash and Credit: An Encyclopedia of Financial Knowledge.** You'll find everything from credit repair to credit reports, balancing a checkbook to budgeting, identity theft to interest rates, and fixing credit to filing bankruptcy. **ASIN: 1985040522**

## Books on Family

**Growing Up Carlisle: Small Town Memories of the 50's & 60's.** This book captures the innocence of a magical time filled with hula- hoops, flat tops and butch wax, glass milk bottles, and little candy buttons stuck on paper rolls. As you journey back to a time that seems so safe, simple, and satisfying, you will begin to relive your own memories and realize the truth of Dr. Seuss' statement, "You will never know the value of a moment until it become a memory." **ASIN: 1501011081**

**The Power of Parents' Words: Sticks and Stones May Break My Bones...**"Our words are powerful! Especially words that parents speak to their children. Those words can single handedly create or crush a child's self-esteem. Since most parents will parent the same way they were parented, we need to make sure we emphasize what our kids are doing right, not just what they are doing wrong. **ASIN: 1503050424**

**How To Turn An Argument Into A Difference of Opinion.** "The main difference between an argument and a difference of opinion can be summed up in one word - EMOTION. Jim offers fifteen practical suggestions on how to keep emotions in check when engaging in a discussion with our mate." **ASIN: 1727493907**

# APPENDIX
## "Ebenezer – Stone of Help"
*"Then Samuel took a stone and set it between Mizpah and Shen, and he named it **Ebenezer (stone of help)**, saying, **"Thus far the Lord has helped us."***
1 Samuel 7:12

When the children of Israel vowed to put away false gods and serve the true God, Samuel told them to gather at Mizpah, and he would intercede for them in prayer. When the Philistines heard that the Jews were gathering like this, they decided it would be a perfect time to attack them and rid them from their land once for all.

As the Philistine armies were drawing near, *"The Lord thundered with a great thunder on that day upon the Philistines and routed them."* (1 Samuel 7:10) This thunder was so loud and so terrifying, it panicked the Philistine armies and they fled in all directions! The Israelites then pursued them and slaughtered them all the way to the city of Bethcar.

To keep this miraculous victory fresh in the minds of the people, Samuel built a stone memorial and called it - **"Ebenezer"** meaning "Stone of Help." An "Ebenezer" serves as a *reminder* of a time when God interjected Himself into our situation and accomplished something that would not have been possible without Him. "Raising our Ebenezer" gives us hope for now, based on a past accomplishment.

Fast forward with me nearly 2,900 years to 1967. Four nations, Egypt, Syria, Iraq, and Jordan have aligned themselves together against the tiny nation of Israel. The president of Iraq declared, *"The existence of Israel is an error which must be rectified. This is our opportunity to wipe out the ignominy, which has been with us since 1948. **Our goal is clear—to wipe Israel off the map."***

God was about to give His people another "Ebenezer!" He interjected Himself into the situation, and although Israel was outnumbered 2 to 1, at the end of the sixth day, Egypt and Syria's Air Force was totally annihilated, Israel tripled the size of its territory, and enough abandoned weapons were recovered to outfit five new Israeli brigades! That event is referred to as "The Six-day War."

When one of the Israeli military Commanders was asked to explain how these miraculous events could have taken place, this was his reply:

*"The God that did, does. The God that was, is."*

That is the meaning of an EBENEZER in a nutshell! What God did for us before, He will do again. Our *past* experience with Him gives us hope for *right now*.

It has been over eight years since the suicide deaths of our two adult children, Shawn, 34, and Melissa, 32. Pondering those dark days are still so overwhelming that I have never been able to read this book once I finished the writing of it.

But there is one thing we know for sure: if it were not for God interjecting Himself into that situation, we would never have made it through the dark valleys. His presence, His peace, and His provision became ours in a way we had never known before, and now it serves to be our "Ebenezer" that gives us hope for today. We believe *"The God that did, does. The God that was, is."* God has earned the right to be trusted.

Dear friend, is there a time in your past that God "interjected" Himself into your situation so He could faithfully bring you through it? Will you now look to Him to use that time as an Ebenezer, "a stone of help," to bring calmness to your chaos and peace to your problems?

If you will, the words of this old hymn, penned in 1758 by Pastor Robert Robinson might well become very precious to you as it is to us. He entitled it: *"Come, Thou Fount of Every Blessing."*

> Come, Thou Fount of every blessing
> Tune my heart to sing Thy grace
> Streams of mercy, never ceasing
> Call for songs of loudest praise.
>
> Teach me some melodious sonnet
> Sung by flaming tongues above
> Praise the mount, I'm fixed upon it
> Mount of Thy redeeming love.
>
> **Here I raise my Ebenezer**
> **Hither by Thy grace I've come**
> And I hope, by Thy good pleasure
> Safely to arrive at home.
>
> Oh, to grace how great a debtor
> Daily I'm constrained to be
> Let that goodness like a fetter
> Bind my wandering heart to Thee
>
> Prone to wander, Lord, I feel it
> Prone to leave the God I love
> Here's my heart, oh, take and seal it
> Seal it for Thy courts above.

———

.

Made in USA - Kendallville, IN
1182439_9781500545581
10.20.2020 0811